UNITED TOWING 1920-90 : A HISTORY

Compiled by Alan Ford

Revised Edition

HUTTON PRESS
1997

Published by the Hutton Press Ltd.
130 Canada Drive, Cherry Burton, Beverley
East Yorkshire HU17 7SB

Copyright © 1990
First published 1990
Revised Edition 1997

Printed by
Burstwick Print & Publicity Services,
13a Anlaby Road, Hull HU1 2PJ

ISBN 1 872167 07 1

CONTENTS

ACKNOWLEDGEMENTS

Thanks are due to the following people for their help and loan of photographs.

Mr. Paul Escreet, Managing Director,
Specialist Marine Services, Hull.
L.E.K.K.O. International Tug Enthusiasts Society
for the Fleet List.
Mr. Michael Lacey.
Imperial War Museum.
John Finch.
Jack Rigg for the Front Cover.
Skyfotos Limited.
Captain E. Johnson.
Captain V. W. Hopper, without whom
this book would not have been completed.

Alan Ford,
Hull,
April 1997.

FOREWORD

This book sets out the history of a company which for seventy years has played a unique role as a part of the British mercantile marine. It is the story of United Towing, the leading ocean towage and salvage company in the United Kingdom, and more importantly it is the story of the 'men' of United Towing, the 'man' tugs and the men who crew them.

The origins of the company can be traced back to 1837 when the first tugs appeared on the River Humber. In 1920 a number of companies operating tugs on the River Humber joined forces and formed United Towing.

Initially the company was only involved in Port, River and Coastal Towage, but in 1925 the first ocean tow was performed, an activity which until then had been the preserve of Dutch Sea-Going Tugs. This first tow was performed by *Seaman*, and was from Boston, Lincolnshire, to Buenos Aires, for the princely sum of £3,600. The records of the company show that this tow generated a profit of £104.

In the intervening years United Towing tugs became a familiar sight on all of the world's oceans, towing ships, barges, dredgers, drydocks and in later years offshore drilling rigs. Apart from commercial towage, United Towing tugs were also involved throughout World War II operating with the Royal Navy and during the two Icelandic 'Cod Wars' when they provided protection to the trawler fleets. They were among the first vessels to be requisitioned for service during the Falklands conflict.

As the years passed the size of the tugs increased to meet the demands of modern shipping and the offshore exploration industry, and this culminated in the delivery in 1980 of *Salvageman*, one of the most powerful ocean-going tugs in the world.

Regrettably the increase in power of the tugs did not lead to an increase in demand for their services, and by the early 1980's the United Towing fleet had been reduced to only three units owing to increased competition from offshore support vessels and the decline in general towage business. In addition a corresponding decline in salvage activity meant that it was no longer economic to maintain tugs on salvage station.

In 1987 a substantial majority interest in United Towing's parent company, North British Maritime Group Ltd., was acquired by Howard Smith Ltd. of Australia. Shortly afterwards the decision was made that the Company should withdraw from the ownership of large ocean-going tugs and concentrate in future on the management of such vessels as well as maintain its salvage expertise.

Throughout its history the Company has enjoyed the closest links with the port of Hull and the vast majority of its personnel have always been recruited from this city. The manning of the tugs has been very much a family business involving fathers, sons, brothers, uncles, cousins and nephews, and today there are tugs and offshore support vessls throughout the world with crew members who began their career on the "Man" tugs of United Towing.

Alan Ford deserves considerable credit for pulling this history together. I know the effort and the hours he has put into this book, diligently researching the records and logbooks of the tugs. Credit must also be given to Arthur Credland, Keeper of Maritime History at the Town Docks Museum in Hull, and to my Secretary Alison Pickard, both of whom gave Alan a great deal of assistance in compiling this history.

I hope all readers, whether associated with United Towing or not, will find this book of interest.

Michael Lacey
Managing Director
United Towing Limited
Hull, January 2nd 1990

M. J. Lacey, Managing Director.

Capt. W. V. Hopper, Warden of Hull Trinity House.

*Wooden-hulled tugs **Hecla** (bt. 1860) and **Lightning** (bt. 1865), of Thomas and John Gray, off Victoria Pier, Hull.*

*Left to right: **Riverman, Welshman, Boatman, Waterman, Motorman** and **Ferryman** c.1930 (the second from left belongs to different owners).*

CHAPTER ONE

THE BEGINNING

The United Towing Co. Ltd. was incoporated on the 29th December 1920 with a merger of the interests of the City Steam Towing Co., T. Gray and Co., the Premier Tug Co. Ltd., T. C. Spink, the Troy Steam Towing Co., S. Harrison and the Humber Steam Towing Co. The signatories to the memorandum of association were H. Dikes, whose status is given as manager, though of which company is not known, W. H. Miller, tug owner, (principal of the Premier Tug Co.), John Robson, tug owner, T. C. Spink, tug owner, R. W. Wheeldon, tug owner, S. Harrison, tug owner and John Watt, shipbroker. This coalition of local towing concerns was prefigured in 1913 by the formation of Hull Associated Tugowners, in response to complaints from the shipping and coal trades regarding the high cost of towage on the Humber. The association offered a reduced tariff conditional upon shipowners contracting towage to them for a period of years and was comprised of T. Gray and Co., the City Towing Co. Ltd. (R. W. Wheeldon), Humber Steam Towing Co., S. Harrison and T. C. Spink which together managed a fleet of twenty-five tugs.

The outbreak of war in August 1914 drastically altered the pattern of trade and the level of activity on the east coast was inevitably reduced by the hostilities, though an increase in naval traffic to some degree compensated for this. Tugs were chartered by the military and naval authorities often to be used as examination vessels or for other defence duties. It was to be some time after the war ended before the level of port traffic built up again and competition between the various local companies for the available customers was intense.

Tug masters found it necessary to take their vessels into the North Sea to pick up incoming ships, a practice known as 'seeking'. They would cruise around in the hope of picking up damaged vessels or a becalmed sailing ship, and without the aid of either radar or radio this could be a fruitless exercise. The result of slack trade and fierce competition was the reason for the decision to rationalise the whole of the Humber towing business by the merging of most of the principal firms into the United Towing Co. Ltd.

Bills of sale were completed between January and May 1921 and the first vessel to enter the fleet was *Muscovite* from the joint ownership of R. W. Wheeldon and John Watt. Though built in 1882 she remained in service with United Towing until 1930, and a further twenty years with John Deheer before being scrapped in 1950. Five other vessels were acquired on the 15th April, registered solely in the name of R. W. Wheeldon; he with Thomas Commander had managed the City Steam Towing Co. On the same day no less than eighteen tugs were transferred from T. Gray and Co. *Mabel* and *Bureaucrat* came to United Towing from T. C. Spink on the 23 March, and the *Autocrat* on the 27 April. The *Tyre* had been purchased from the Troy Steam Towing Co. on 2 March and seven further craft passed from the Premier Tug Co. between the 14 April and 7 May. There were thus five principal contributors from local firms, and in addition the *Victor* was bought from a firm in Bridgewater on 2 May. In the first year of operation the United Towing Co. therefore had a total of thirty-six vessels at its command.

Thomas Clarkson Spink, previously manager of the Hull Associated Tug Owners, was appointed managing director, a post he retained for some forty years. Also on the board of directors was Robert Walker Wheeldon who had started work at the age of eleven and began his long connection with the towing business at fifteen as an engineer's apprentice. Active in local politics he was chairman of the Property and Bridges Committee, deputy chairman of the Transport Committee and elected an Alderman in 1930. In the same year he became sheriff, and was mayor of Hull in 1931.

The new company had as its headquarters premises at 11 Nelson Street, overlooking the Humber at Victoria pier, which had previously been occupied by the Hull Associated Tug Owners. The various towing companies which preceded the amalgamation had all been clustered within a small compass between High Street and the Town Docks: Premier Tug Co. at 3 Nelson Street, City Steam Towing Co. Minerva Pier, and T. Gray and Co. at 4 Colonial Chambers, Princes Dock Side and Wellington Street west, with additional premises at Alexandra Dock. Troy Steam Towing Co. were at 36 High Street and only the Humber Steam Towing Co., (manager S. Harrison) were away from this nexus, at 337 Hedon Road. After the merger only two independent companies remained, Fosters (5 Wellington Street and Humber Dock Street) with four small, low-powered vessels and Thompson (7 Pier Street) with eight craft of varying size and quality.

Another vessel owned by the Premier Tug Co., apart from the seven mentioned above, the *Rose Ann* is credited to United Towing by Lloyds in 1922-3 but for her last entry in 1923-4 ownership is again given to W. H. Miller manager of the Premier Tug Co. Built in 1879 she was acquired from H. M. Grayson and Co. in 1918 by the Hull firm but remained on the register at Douglas, Isle of Man.

During and after the war barge-towing on the Humber and the large associated network of rivers and canals provided a significant proportion of the tug operators revenue. A special department was established to deal with the upriver work provided by barge-towing contracts and in July 1921 the *Dalesman* was repaired and put into service on the upper Trent to work there on a permanent basis. During the severe Autumn drought the drop in water level resulted in a broken propeller and damaged shaft.

The new company was engaged in the whole gamut of local harbour work, docking cargo vessels, shifting them in the confines of the docks, and dry-docking. Many jobs were still found by 'seeking' the practise of meeting vessels downriver or in the approaches when the master of the tug would negotiate a price with the captain. Sailing vessels, including grain ships from Australia, were still arriving in the United Kingdom and the competition was very keen with a fee of £118 asked for towing the *Carnmoney* from Downs to Goole and £200 for bringing *Nordfarer* from Downs to Hull.

During the herring season the coal barges *King Coal* and *Coalman* followed the fleet as they moved south from Shetland, hauled by United vessels which took them to Blyth or the Tyne for refilling as needed. The *King Coal* appears regularly in the records towed between Goole and Lowestoft and the *Emily Smeed* and *Wynyard Park* between Boston and Lowestoft. The coal barges *Melba* and *Moonland* were frequently taken from the Tyne to Calais and Dunkirk. Indeed barges were the staple of sea-towing at the time and were taken all over the North Sea and to and from northern France. In April 1922 *Autocrat* lost two of her three charges in heavy weather between London and Bristol. Providing for its own fleet the company's coal hulk *Josva* was tied up on the river Hull but since they did not have their own berth there were frequent complaints of obstruction by other craft seeking moorings. Later the *James Watt* replaced her as the company hulk.

In December 1922 the company resolved that all new vessels would be named with a *-man* suffix establishing for the whole fleet the custom that had prevailed in Gray's before amalgamation. During the summer months Gray's *Frenchman* had been used as an excursion vessel taking holiday makers, up to 246 at a time, for trips out of Bridlington harbour. This practice also continued and in 1928 when the *Yorkshireman* was built she took over the seaside cruises and the *Frenchman* was employed for short trips on the Humber. The next year however the London North Eastern Railway Company started running their ferries for excursions at half the price and the old faithful *Frenchman*, by then thirty-seven years old, was stripped down and moored as a coal hulk for United at Church Lane Staith. There she remained until diesel-powered vessels replaced the steam tugs and she

Muscovite.

Tyre.

13

Alderman Robert Walter Wheeldon, J.P.

R. W. Wheeldon.

283 · Bridlington · Steamer Entering The Harbour

Frenchman entering Bridlington Harbour.

Yorkshireman with passengers aboard.

was finally towed to New Holland for scrap in 1963.

The older tugs were sold off and a rebuilding programme began, partly stimulated by a complaint from Ellerman's Wilson Line that United Towing's vessels were too small to handle their steamers. The *Superman* was delivered in April 1923 and her sister ship the *Masterman* soon followed, both from the Selby yard of Messrs. Cochranes. Each vessel was over 96 feet long at a cost of £5,980 for the hull and £5,760 for the engines (built by Earles of Hull), each developing 763 i.h.p. In the same month the *Berty* (ex- Premier Tug Co.) built in 1914 was sold to Portuguese owners for £3,500 and the *Aquila* for £1600 to local rivals, Fosters. Early in 1924 *Pioneer* and *Themis* were also sold to their rivals, for a total of £7000 and with this cash United Towing purchased 701 of a total of 1401 Fosters shares giving them a controlling interest. Only Thompsons then remained as local competition and a few months prior to this move they had circulated a letter to various shipowners intimating that United Towing were gaining a virtual monopoly. They also claimed the board of directors was made up of people who had other shipping interests in the port and were stifling a healthy competitive atmosphere. Once they were aware of the contents of the letter United Towing were able to reply in a circular to local shipping firms giving their own interpretation of the situation and explanation of the cost of towing services.

The company was also making a good return from salvage operations both within the Humber estuary and outside, though the lack of radio meant that the reports of strandings without the river had to be relayed by telephone on the shore or by messages passed from incoming vessels. The *Hullman* was the first of the fleet to be fitted with radio, installed by the Marconi company in April 1924. *Tradesman* and *Headman*, then building, were also to have wireless sets and a wireless operator became part of the crew of all vessels so equipped. Robert Holmes was Engineer Superintendent at the time, known for his strong religious principles, as well as being an able engineer and naval architect. When the second order for

new tugs had been given the company had contemplated fitting Welin boat davits but these proved too expensive and Holmes designed and patented a type of davit which eventually entered into general service throughout the fleet. The principle of the mechanism was a single horizontal hand wheel with a spindle vertically geared to a longitudinal shaft which linked both the forward and after davits allowing one man to turn out both at the same time. Restructuring continued with the sale of the *Victor* for £300 to a scrapyard at Felixstowe in January 1924 and in the course of the year *Tradesman* and *Headman* entered service to enable the company to expand its zone of operations into the Mediterranean and the north Atlantic.

The need for bigger tugs to meet the requirements of larger cargo vessels was still evident and the company also had ambitions to extend their business into ocean towage. A large sea-going tug to be known as the *Seaman* was put on the drawing board and Cochranes of Selby received the contract to build a vessel 125 feet long with 28 foot beam and a triple expansion steam engine developing around 1100 i.h.p. Already in 1923 the *Hullman* (built 1914) had towed the trawler *St. Hubert* from Murmansk to Hull in a round voyage of twenty-six days which yielded £750 in fees.

The *Lady Bute* built in 1857 was sold as scrap for £100 and in December 1924 *Powerful* and *Blighty* were disposed of for £60 and £100 respectively. In the same month *Seaman* was delivered from the builder's yard at Selby following the *Headman* and *Tradesman* which had been completed in the summer. In May 1925 *Seaman* gained her first ocean tow, to take two ex-naval minesweepers, the *Stepdance* and *Quadrille* from Boston, Lincs., to Buenos Aires, a contract worth £3,600. They left England on the 16 May, 1925, but unfortunately *Stepdance* foundered in a storm in the Bay of Biscay. After repairs to the remaining vessel at Gijon *Seaman* continued on her way with a stop for coal at St. Vincent, Cape Verde, on the 30 June, before finally reaching Argentina. Setting back on the 14 August she arrived in

Hull on 17 September after a total of 124 days at sea. The net profit was only £140, but all concerned had gained invaluable experience for the future.

Masterman, though only two years old, was sold in February 1925 to a Thames tug company for £12,900 and this transaction no doubt helped to build up capital for the takeover of Thompson Towage in November of the following year. The whole fleet was purchased outright and with this move the only remaining independent towing company in the port was eleminated. Four of the Thompson vessels, *Scotsman*, *Terrier*, *Alexandra* and *Romulus* were sold for scrap to Henry Scarr of Hessle and the names of the other four were changed, *Traho* to *Riverman*, *Tormentor* to *Ferryman*, *Sindia* to *Tribesman* and *Torris* to *Pressman*.

Two new vessels *Prizeman* and *Nobleman*, each developing 800 i.h.p., were delivered in November and December of 1925. Then in Spring of the following year *Tyre*, *Norman*, *Orion* and *Winchester* all went for scrap and the tug *Irishman* was sold for £675 to John Deheer, the local barge owner.

To provide another tug to work the river Trent in 1927 the engine and boiler were taken out of the *Fenman* and put into a new hull named *Boatman*; the shell of *Fenman* was sold for £150. The service provided by United Towing was evidently reliable and priced at a sensible level since the Trent Navigation requested the company to take over all towage on the canal between Newark and Nottingham. At the end of the year *Muscovite* was chartered to John Deheer for a six week period and some of the older elements of the fleet were disposed of in 1928. *Hullman* went to the Anticosti Shipping Co. of Montreal but was damaged on passage to Quebec in an encounter with field ice. The *Stephen Gray*, a paddle tug built in 1887, was sold to T. Ward of Inverkeithing for a scrap price of £200 including delivery. The *Superman* built only five years previously went to an Argentinian firm for £11,750 as did the *Tradesman* in the same year. These sales helped to purchase two new tugs *Irishman* and *Scotsman* delivered in the Spring of 1929 and an order was placed in June for a 62 foot twin-screw motor tug, to be named *Waterman*.

May 1928 saw the appearance of *Yorkshireman* a twin-screw tug of shallow draught built for the dual purpose of towing and passenger carrying. She was flat-bottomed to allow her to use Bridlington harbour without getting stuck in the mud and to make her particularly useful for assisting and refloating stranded vessels. It was easy for her to move in close to a stricken craft though after making a connection the towing wire might be passed to a more powerful tug. An agreement was reached with the Bridlington Harbour Commissioners in 1929 and £150 was paid for the next five years to cover harbour dues and all charges for the summer season of excursions. *Yorkshireman* saw great service and became one of the best known of all craft in the north east until the fleet was totally converted to diesel power and she ceased operating. After giving pleasure to many thousands of seaside visitors she was towed, in August 1965, by *Workman* to Boom in Belgium.

The *Scotsman* towed the four-masted ship *Garthpool* from Cobh (Queenstown) to Hull in June 1929 and in October *Seaman* took her into the English channel as far as Beachy Head. As it turned out both tugs were playing their part in an historic voyage for when she foundered on a reef off Bona Vista Island, Cape Verde, she proved to be the last full-rigged ship to fly the red ensign. Many of the crew were from Yorkshire and included a number of men gaining their sailing time which was then still necessary to qualify as an accredited Humber pilot. Fortunately there were no casualties other than the ship itself.

After the general strike of 1926 the trade recession continued to a lessening degree until the outbreak of the Second World War. The large and versatile United Towing fleet was able, however, to tackle an immense variety of jobs, covering the whole range from harbour duties to ocean-towing. Recovering anchors and cables lost from the extensive fleets of Hull and Grimsby trawlers was a regular souce of income. Not infrequently fishing vessels needed assistance getting off a sand or mud bank in the Humber or after being stranded on the east coast. Towing Thames barges constructed on the Trent and its connecting waterways was a recurring job. They were taken from Gainsborough as far as Hull Roads then rigged with lights and towing bridles by the crew of a sea tug which towed them, usually in groups of three, down to the Thames. These tows kept the small crew well occupied and their final task before returning home was to retrieve the lights and towing gear.

Fire-fighting was yet another task in which tugs played a significant role. The *Biddy* helped to protect the trawlers berthed in St. Andrew's Dock during the fire in September 1929 which destroyed most of the newly built dockside installations. *Biddy* was in action again the following month along with *Pinky* during a fire at Saltend and these two together with the *Norman* and *Marksman* salvaged the ss *Aberhill* in August 1930 after a serious collision.

Seaman was despatched on the terms of Lloyd's 'open form' to assist a Latvian steamer ss *Everline* (built in 1899) which had lost her propeller in a gale ninety miles off Shetland. Meanwhile a trawler had carried a line to the vessel but the cable parted and despite the deployment of a sea anchor she drifted to within two miles of the shore. The Lerwick lifeboat took off the crew of the *Everline* and upon the arrival of *Seaman* the trawler crew once again managed to get a line aboard the steamer and she was then towed safely down to the Tyne. In Spring of the same year *Norman* with *Cyclope*, a dipper dredger, in tow from the Tyne to Havre, were struck by hurricane force winds off the Holderness coast. The dredger was lost and pieces of wreckage later washed up on the beach at Holmpton.

When a vessel stranded it often took a great deal of pulling power to refloat her. The *Seaman* and three Dutch tugs were all employed in hauling the ss *Zembra* off the Haisbro Sands in November 1931, and four United craft, *Seaman*, *R. W. Wheeldon*, *Headman* and *Nobleman*, refloated ss *Bravo* aground at Easington in the following year. Attempts made over a period of three days in September 1932 enabled *Riverman*, *Boatman*, *Tollman* and *Waterman* to bring off the ss *Border Firth* and the company received £650 plus costs for their services. In May 1933 no less than six tugs, *Seaman*, *Superman*, *Scotsman*, *Norman*, *Irishman* and *Nobleman* were involved in refloating the tanker *San Fabian* when she grounded below Saltend whilst approaching the jetty to berth.

Despite the general economic gloom the fleet was kept up to scratch by a continuing policy of scrapping and renewal. The ancient *Acor*, built in 1897, was sold to T. Ward of Inverkeithing for breaking at a price of £440, including delivery, and the tug *Finlay* was sold as a working vessel to the Boston Dock and Harbour Commission for £2000. *Kinsman* went to J. P. Knight of London in 1930 for £2,800 and *Tribesman* to a French firm at Le Havre for £3,500. The hulk *James Watt* was disposed of to Lincoln and Hull Water Transport for a mere £20 her place being taken by *Frenchman*. In 1931 the same company also purchased the hulk *Josva* for £1 plus £5 for delivery to Owston Ferry! The same year United Towing purchased the premises at 60-1 High Street along with the river frontage which gave a permanent berth for *Frenchman* at Chapel Lane Staithe. Staff occupied the building from 5 June 1931, but modifications were not completed until 1937.

A new upriver tug of shallow draft, the *Waterman*, had been delivered in February 1930 and *Hillman* was completed by Henry Scarr of Hessle in July. The latter firm was then given an order for a 75 foot tug, suitable for use on the lower Trent which was delivered in May the following year and given the name *Tollman*.

After asking for tenders for an ocean-going tug with a length of 120 feet, the managing director T. C. Spink awarded the order to Cochranes of Selby in December 1932. Ready in the following April the *Superman* developed 900 hp with a maximum speed of more than 11 knots. The specification included teak decks and an Oertz rudder.

Dalesman.

Hullman.

Seaman with *Stepdance* and *Quadrille.*

Boatman.

Seaman towing four-master **Parma**.

The age of sail was not finished and grain ships still came into the Humber. In June 1933 the barks *Olivebank* and *Parma* were towed into Hull from the North Sea having been picked up by the traditional method of seeking. Before the end of the month their cargoes had been discharged and they were ready to be towed out to sea again. Another of the famous fleet known as the flying 'Ps', the bark *Pommern* and the four-masted barkentine *Mozart* were picked up in the summer of 1934 and were under tow for a full day before arriving at Alexandra Dock. The Swedish bark *C. B. Pedersen* was connected at Smiths Knoll soon after.

Vessels frequently stranded in the Humber, especially in the autumn and winter, as will be obvious from the incidents already recalled. Movement of traffic on the river was controlled with the aid of inadequate wireless communications and radar had yet to be invented. In September 1933 *Guardsman*, *Irishman*, and *Prizeman* freed a loaded timber vessel aground on the Middle Sand whilst *Superman* and *Autocrat* refloated *m.v. Vivi* ashore near Killingholme. Sometimes even the tugs found themselves in trouble and in July 1934 whilst assisting the Goole tug *Salvage* to refloat ss *Ouse* near Whitton, *Autocrat* got across the tide, was pulled over and sank. The crew were saved and *Autocrat* was eventually raised by F. Hall and Co. to be reconditioned ready for service less than two months later.

A tug master might happen across a job whilst on passage as when the *Seaman* steaming from Hull to Faroes came upon the ss *Cairnglen* aground at Huna in the Pentland Firth. She assisted the tug *Oxcar* of the Leith Salvage and Towage Co. Ltd. and after lightening her load the general cargo vessel of over 5,000 tons was refloated and towed to Leith by *Seaman*, *Scotsman* and *Norman*.

On 9th January 1935 tragedy overtook the Hull trawler *Edgar Wallace* as she made for the entrance to St. Andrew's Dock. Caught by the tide, she was driven upriver towards Hessle, hit a sand bank and overturned with the death of fifteen of her eighteen man crew. In the subsequent salvage operation the tragedy was compounded when one of the lifting lighters dragged her anchor and fouled the wreck and the *Boatman* capsized across the tide. The tug engineer trapped underneath was drowned. Eventually the *Boatman*, floating bottom up, was taken in tow by *Waterman* and *Tollman* and beached at Hessle. Continuous westerly gales and strong tides made further activity hazardous and attempts at salvage were finally abandoned on 21 March.

Evidently *Yorkshireman* was still doing good business with the trippers at two shillings a head and the company towed a small dredger to Bridlington to ensure a good level bottom for her summer berth. The Australian grain ships continued to sail into the port giving the towing industry useful revenue and adding a touch of romance to the port. Sight of these last representatives of the great fleets of sailing ships always created a stir among the idlers at Victoria Pier, and in the summer of 1935 both the German barque *Priwall* and the *Archibald Russell* made an appearance.

An impressive ocean tow of 115 days was undertaken by *Seaman* starting out from Bahia Blanca on 26 March 1936 with the cruiser *Garibaldi*. Whilst on passage to Copenhagen the old warship was sold to shipbreakers at Blyth where she was delivered on 11 June having been hauled a distance of 6,843 miles. During the summer, *Southern Cross*, *Krooman* and *Dalesman* were all sold for scrap and *Handyman* followed in November. *Nobleman* was purchased by Falmouth Towage Co. in May 1937 and renamed *Fairnilee*. The m.t. *Hillman* was sold to Venezuelan Oil Development of London and the *Pressman* to French interests in Oran, North Africa in October 1938. Cochranes were given an order for a large sea-going tug in January 1937. Named *Englishman* she was 135 feet long with a beam of 30 feet and fitted with engines by C. D. Holmes developing 1250 i.h.p. A special salvage pump was fitted and she also was provided with a small motor boat. Capable of pulling 13½ tons she reached a speed of over 12 knots. *Boatman* was re-engined with a six cylinder Deutz diesel though the wholesale conversion of the fleet to diesel power did not take place until long after the war.

The management was approached by the Transport and General Workers Union with the aim of establishing union representation for the work force. Negotiations for greater job security and improved pay at a time when trade was on the upturn broke down and a strike began on 17 September, 1937, which was joined by all except the masters and a handful of crew members. Through the intervention of the Shipping Committee of the Hull Chamber of Commerce a new pay scale was formulated and work resumed again a month later on 17 October. Earlier the same year the company had decided to make provision for long-serving employees who had been forced to retire through ill-health and were living on limited means. Payments from five shillings to a pound per week were agreed according to individual circumstances though the total disbursements from the company's funds were not to exceed £500 in any year.

The sea tugs did a lot of work for shipbreaking yards in 1937; the yards of T. W. Ward at Briton Ferry, Swansea Bay, and Pembroke Dock, Milford Haven being particularly busy at this period, but occasionally small craft were towed to Ward's yard at Hoyle near St. Ives. Most of the yards concernd could only accept delivery on the spring tides and even visits to Messrs. John Cashmore, Newport, Monmouth, were not without difficulty. Quite large vessels can penetrate the Usk but deliveries to their yard had to be timed very critically to arrive on the berth at high tide.

On 10 April 1937, *Seaman*, *Superman*, *Irishman*, *Nobleman* and *Prizeman* all steamed up to Rosyth to berth the ss *Caledonia* (ex-*Majestic*) for which a fee of £935 was received.

Anchored in dense fog off Lee-on-Solent the *Prizeman* was run down by the *Hantonia* (1560 tons), a steamer belonging to the Southern Railway Co. Fortunately there was no loss of life and one of her two companions *Irishman* was able to beach her. After inspection at Southampton it was decided to tow her to Hull for reconditioning. Foul weather in January and February 1938 resulted in a whole catalogue of incidents on the Humber. Two trawlers grounded in the river, two barges stranded at Sammy's Point, and a steamer went ashore on the Haile Sand. On the seaward side of Spurn ss *King Edgar* drove onto the Binks, a notorious graveyard for ships through the centuries, and a destroyer grounded at Scarborough. All of these casualties were attended by United Towing craft.

In June 1937 *Seaman* towed a Brazilian coastal defence vessel from Rio de Janeiro to La Spezia in Italy and in the following month *Superman* towed the cruiser *Barroso* from Rio de Janeiro to La Spezia. A new *Krooman* was delivered in January 1938 with a sister vessel named *Brahman*, both constructed at Cochranes Selby yard.

War clouds wre gathering and the increased naval activity all helped to provide more work. *Scotsman* with a minelayer in tow from Portsmoth to Newport in January 1939 ran into a north-west gale off Trevose Head. The minelayer drove ashore and one of the 'run' crew of four was swept overboard and lost.

CHAPTER TWO

THE SECOND WORLD WAR

On the outbreak of hostilities the *Yorkshireman's* summer season at Bridlington was curtailed and she arrived back in Hull on 4 September 1939. Even so her earnings were more than for the previous year, as if holidaymakers were having a final fling before the inevitable happened. Mr. Spinks, managing director and still very much in command, informed his board that the Port Emergency committee had formed a sub-committee with him as chaiman and the company's office as headquarters to deal with all aspects of towage and control of tug movements in the Humber., This had been decided even before war had been declared but until then the contingency plans remained a close secret. A large number of craft were requisitioned by the Ministry of Shipping, leaving United Towing to provide an efficient service, whether for up-river towing or allocating sea tugs for casualties in the estuary, with a much reduced fleet. *Brahman* was commissioned by the navy at Rosyth and her name changed to *Bat* to prevent any confusion with *Barham* even though the latter was a battleship! *Yorkshireman* herself was requisitioned by the government on 6 October followed by *Superman* on 1 November. The Director of Sea Transport sent them to various ports to be used for towage services and as examination vessels, or placed them on rescue station. *Krooman* and *Norman* followed *Brahman* to Rosyth, *Guardsman* and *Roman* were put in the examination service at Southend, *Englishman* in the rescue service at Campbeltown and Milford haven, whilst *Yorkshireman*, *Superman*, *Seaman* and *Ferryman* were all posted to Grimsby, though the last two were soon to be used as ocean rescue tugs.

In the Spring insurance cover of £52,000 had been taken out with Lloyds for the three large tugs *Englishman*, *Superman* and *Seaman*, but when the company endeavoured to obtain war risk cover the premiums were prohibitively high. The rates quoted were 1% of the value per month with movement confined to home waters or 2% of the value for three months with the same restrictions. The remainder of the fleet were covered by a combination of marine insurance companies but for the early part of hostilities none of the vessels was protected by a war risk policy.

On 4 November the m.v. *Canada*, damaged in action, founded off the estuary after four tugs had been despatched to help her. Six tugs went to the aid of ss *Deerpool* aground on the Binks on the 13th of the month and two days later the steamer *Georgis* ran on to the wreck of the *Canada*, and also the very same day *Pilendsir* foundered off the Humber light vessel. The approaches to the Humber were a prize target for German mines and air attacks and when barrage balloons were moored in the river tugs were used to transport crews and equipment.

On 1 December 1939 Port Tariffs were increased by 25% and on the following day *Seaman* was requisitioned, which meant that almost all the sea-going fleet had been taken. The tugs remaining were worked very hard indeed and the burden fell not only on a fleet depleted in numbers but also by loss of experienced masters and crews. Some of these were put in charge of tugs of the Royal Naval Fleet Auxillary which built up a useful squadron of ocean-going tugs. Initially oil-fired steamers, they were superseded by a series of 1100 ton craft, 200 feet long which developed 400 HP and were fitted with towing wires.

A vast roll call of war casualties were attended by the remaining United tugs, such as *San Delfino*, *British Triumph*. *Royal Crown*, *British Councillor*, *Sagacity*, *Robrix*, *Essex Lance*, *Aroma*, *Cormarsh*, *Chance*, *Dalewood*, *Eaglescliff Hall*, *Afterglow*, *Eastwood*, *Empire Sedge* and *Empire Flaminian* as well as the tug *Varro* with a number of unexploded bombs on board. The steamer *Lornaston* after leaving Hull developed engine trouble

Tollman *towing trawler fitted with 'hammer' device on bows to detonate acoustic mines.*

*Naval tug W44, **Seaman** (bt. 1924).*

*Naval tug W89, **Superman** (bt. 1933).*

*Envoy class naval tug **Enchanter** which became **Englishman** in 1947.*

Captain O. V. Jones in 1941 wearing his OBE.

Englishman, *formerly the naval tug* **Enchanter**.

Serviceman, *formerly the* **Empire Stella**.

east-south-east of the Humber light vessel and was towed to Albert Dock by *Irishman* and *Bureaucrat* after first anchoring in Hawke roads and calling at Immingham. The *Merman* and *Marksman* recovered the anchor and chain of the destroyer *Greyhound* and HMS *Express*, damaged and in tow of a destroyer was taken in charge by *Irishman* and *R. W. Wheeldon* from Spurn light vessel. They towed her into Hull where she was berthed at King George Dock. For a period of two months in the spring of 1940 *R. W. Wheeldon* was hired by the Ministry of Shipping and at about the same time the Admiralty Salvage office claimed the use of several rooms in the company's offices. HMS *Vega* was picked up from a navy tug at the Humber light vessel by the busy *R. W. Wheeldon* and *Prizeman*, and HMS *Ripley*, stranded at North Landing, Flamborough was refloated and hauled to Grimsby by *Prizeman* and *Scotsman*. The mine-sweeper *Borde* was brought in from the Humber light ship and during numerous air raids on the Hull docks United Towing vessels were always ready to fight fires and move endangered ships from their moorings. Meanwhile a busy building programme got under way to meet the ever increasing demand for replacement harbour tugs and control tugs. Many of the latter were put under the management of United Towing and like most of the ministry tugs were given names prefixed *Empire*, usually in combination with a boy's or girl's name.

During the first four months of hostilities the company's tugs, plant and staff were included in various salvage operations which had to remain secret and often were not recorded. A job which does appear in the work books however is the refloating of the 1729 ton collier ss *Corbrook* south of Cromer by *Prizeman*, assisted by a small tug and the local lifeboat. This was the first salvage recorded on Lloyds 'Open Form' since the outbreak of war and the company received £2,750 plus £110 for loss of gear. The value of *Corbrook* and her cargo was £35,000. An award of £2,750 was made in June 1940 refloating the ss *Bilton* after she had caught fire in the William Wright dock but the waters of the North Sea were just as dangerous to tugs as any other vessel and on 15 November 1940 the *Guardsman* was sunk by a mine off the North Foreland.

On 31 January 1941, a Latvian steamer the ss *Trautmilla* was stranded offshore at Walcott near Cromer after being bombed and abandoned by her crew. *Irishman* and *Bureaucrat* pulled her off and brought her safe into Great Yarmouth for which an £8,000 salvage fee was earned.

United Towing continued to make its own contribution to the development of tug design and Robert Holmes prepared plans for two oil-fired steam tugs, similar to the steamer *Englishman*, but with certain improvements. They would be built at Goole for the Board of Trade and the company sought a declaration that nothing would be done with these tugs after the war to prejudice their trading position. Shortly after when the Board of Trade was absorbed by the Ministry of Shipping and all shipbuilding was put under the control of the Admiralty they requested Holmes' designs and specifications for the 100 foot tugs to be handed over. The two vessels completed at Goole in the Summer of 1941 were named *Empire Larch* and *Empire Oak* and immediately placed under the management of United Towing. Sadly on 22 August, less than two months after completion, the *Empire Oak* was torpedoed and sunk whilst in convoy off south-west Portugal with the loss of fourteen men out of a crew of twenty. Her master Captain F. E. Christian later commanded her sister ship which was bought by the company after the war and named *Masterman*. Tugs were allocated to them from other companies too including the *Empire Henchman*, formerly *Karl* of the Gothenburg Salvage and Towage Co., and *Queens Cross* from Robinson and Crossthwaite at Middlesbrough; *Kings Cross* came from the same company in June 1941.

Small craft like tugs were very exposed out at sea and on 10 July 1941 *Seaman*, some 290 miles west of Ireland, was surprised by a Focke-Wolf Condor aircraft. She pressed home three attacks, but determined work at the

Lewis gun by the mate J. Ryan brought her down. Three of the aircrew were killed and three others were picked up and taken prisoner. Captain O. V. Jones, master, was given the OBE (C.D.), Ryan received the George Medal and seaman G. Suddaby was commended for good service. After the war, Captain Jones entered the pilot service and eventually became Master Warden of Hull Trinity House. This was a hectic period of the war and on the 22nd of the same month *Englishman*, forty miles west of Tory Island in the north-west approaches, was attacked and sunk by another enemy plane. The master and all her crew were lost. The tug *Brahman* gave invaluable help to the navy, and in August 1941 was despatched from Rosyth to assist the destroyer *Kelly*, badly damaged during the evacuation of Norway under the command of Lord Mountbatten. This time she reached home safely but on 23 May 1941 she was bombed and sunk by enemy aircraft at the battle of Crete. During the Hull Blitz life was just as dangerous on shore and staff were kept busy during the air raids which so badly mauled the old town area. On 21 January 1941, the company's warehouse at the rear of 61 High Street was taken over by H.M. Office of Works and early next year the efforts of United Towing personnel were brought to the attention of the Duke of Kent who visited the city on 2 February 1942. At the express request of the Flag officer of the Humber, Mr. Thomas Spinks and seven members of staff were presented to his royal highness.

The events recalled above could be repeated many times over with different tugs, different places and United Towing continued to play a crucial role in maritime activities on the Humber whilst their personnel and vessels were also active all round the British Isles.

The war also brought about another 'rationalisation' of the fleet. After gaining a controlling interest in Fosters tugs, two of their vessels *Seeker* and *Aquila* formed the nucleus of a harbour tug fleet in a new company established in 1927 and entitled Humber Tugs Ltd. Under United's control though, the finances were kept entirely separate. *Aquila* received severe damage in an air-raid and was sold for scrap, then United Towing purchased *Seeker* for £600.

Eventually the allies were able to contemplate the invasion of Europe to be launched onto the Normandy coast on 6 June 1944. A number of massive engineering projects formed part of the preparations, notably Pluto ('pipe line under the ocean') for supplying fuel to the armed forces as soon as they landed and the remarkable Mulberry harbour. It was absolutely essential if the large numbers of men with all their vehicles and stores were to gain a bridgehead that a secure anchorage be provided for the supply ships. The Mulberry was an artificial harbour constructed of numerous concrete units which after assembly all round the coast had then to be towed to their positions opposite the invasion beaches. United Towing tugs and craft managed by them played a large part in moving the Pluto pipe spools and Mulberry units. They also helped to shepherd fleets of landing craft and position various obsolete ships which were sunk near the landing points to act as breakwaters.

Some awards to United's personnel have been mentioned already but we must also record the MBE given to Captain James Richardson for bringing HMS *Kelly* safely into harbour. He was also mentioned in despatches in February 1945.

Captain William Gardiner, master of the tug *Empire Jonathan*, was also given the MBE for towing an ammunition barge off a blazing quayside during the struggle to establish a port when our troops were advancing through Belgium.

CHAPTER THREE

PEACE and PROSPERITY

When hostilities ceased the requisitioned tugs were returned to their owners and the Ministry of War Transport had a large number of craft which they offered for sale. In order to re-establish the fleet as quickly as possible and take advantage of the expected peace-time boom United Towing acquired a selection of these. The ocean tug *Empire Larch* was renamed *Masterman* and four others, *Empire Clara*, which became *Airman, Empire Vera, Empire Stella* and *Empire Nina* were renamed *Rifleman, Serviceman* and *Guardsman* respectively. The last were all of the same class, with a flush deck 116 feet long and 296 tons gross. Their oil-fired, triple expansion steam engines generated 700 h.p. which meant they were rather underpowered, but a low rate of consumption and tanks capable of holding 172 tons of fuel enabled them to tow small craft for fairly long distances. *Airman, Rifleman, Serviceman* and *Guardsman* were used as harbour tugs when not sea-towing, chiefly as head tugs for vessels in King George dock and for manoeuvering tankers at the oil jetties. Two large ocean tugs were also purchased from the Ministry, *Empire Bess*, renamed *Merchantman* and *Empire Julia* which joined the fleet as *Tradesman*. Both of the same class they were 137 feet long, 592 tons gross and developed 1350 h.p. Triple expansion engines and a fuel capacity of 329 tons, enabled them to stay at sea for up to 45 days and they built up a sound reputation as ocean plodders. Neither of these vessels had towing winches, and so all towing was done from a hook. Purchased in 1947 the *Enchanter* was named *Englishman*, a fine looking vessel 164 feet long and 716 tons gross. Her hull design made her a first class sea tug and with two boilers she could achieve 1800 h.p. She also used a towing hook and required a tow rope of 20″

circumference, her gear being handled by a capstan on the after deck. Three T.I.D tugs also joined United Towing, representatives of a class of pre-fabricated, all-welded craft pioneered by Richard Dunston of Thorne. These particular examples named, *Yeoman, Bowman* and *Fenman* were extensively rebuilt and the bow remodelled. Coal-burning with two-cylinder engines they were 73 feet long, 55 tons gross, and developed 260 h.p.

The early post-war period was a very busy time for United Towing with ports and approaches being cleared of wrecks and lifting craft requiring to be moved around. There was very little continental competition at the time and the company's vessels were to be found actively engaged off the coast of Norway and in the Baltic. Obsolete vessels which had been scuttled near the Normandy beaches were being patched up and re-floated. Facilities were poor, although the Mulberry harbours provided a base to work from to make them sea-worthy before towing to the breakers. The ballast had frequently shifted and they were heavily waterlogged so that at least one of these vessels sank and they would often arrive at their destination with a serious list. One of the earliest ocean tows immediately post-war was the movement of the 4189 ton Elder Dempster steamer *Sangara* from Lagos to the Tyne by *Seaman* which bunkered at Freetown, St. Vincent, Las Palmas, and Falmouth *en route*. Surplus landing craft were being disposed of by the government and acquired for conversion to ferries, coastal traders and a large variety of purposes. Purchasers all over Europe, and even further afield, sought the services of tug operators to deliver them to their destinations. In July 1946 *Masterman* and *Merchantman* each took two landing craft from Harwich to Alexandria in Egypt. After safe arrival they continued through the Suez canal to pick up a badly damaged tanker from Massawa and tow her to Genoa. The tanker, a Norwegian vessel called *Erling Brovig*, broke in two the day after leaving Massawa and the tugs with one section each finally made a 'safe' delivery in Italy.

Hull was busy as an embarkation port for service

personnel going over to Germany as garrison troops for the British Army of the Rhine and the two transport vessels *Empire Rapier* and *Empire Halberd* were a familiar sight sailing to and from Cuxhaven. In September 1946 *Tradesman* and *Superman* each took a rocket-launching craft from the Humber to Oslo before proceeding to Gothenburg to tow the tanker *Polycarp* from there to Rotterdam. She had been converted for use as a refuelling depot ship and accommodation for U-boat crews, but had been torpedoed by the British laying open her engine room to the sea. During December 1946 a Shell tanker *Kelletia* which had been under tow in the English Channel got into trouble and was taken into Southampton where the two United Towing vessels *Merchantman* and *Tradesman* completed her voyage to the Tyne. In the same month the same two tugs hauled *Argus*, the first British aircraft carrier, from Chatham to Inverkeithing. At the beginning of 1947 *Tradesman*, after escorting the British India *Durenda* from Hull to London, then towed a tug *Empire Cedar* on the return journey to Hull. She was reconditioned and modified to enter the United Towing fleet as *Handyman*.

In February and March, three destroyers of the US Navy were towed from Hartlepool to Piraeus, by *Merchantman*, *Tradesman* and *Serviceman*. In each, the anchor cable of the warship was used as a towing bridle but proved to be almost worn through. The chain of the *Serviceman's* tow parted during heavy weather in the Bay of Biscay though the connection was recovered and all three destroyers were eventually docked in Greece. *Merchantman* carried on through the Suez canal to Bombay where she picked up a tanker, the *Empire Thane*, on 20 April and brought her to a berth in Falmouth some three months later on 16 July. *Masterman* towed ss *Orata* from Ponta Delgada in the Azores to Genoa and during May and June 1947 *Tradesman* and *Masterman* each took a large landing craft from Leith to Rio de Janeiro. On the way home the *Tradesman* picked up a Shell tank barge in St. Vincent, Cape Verde Islands, and towed it to the Tyne, whilst the *Masterman*, after completing the previous task in Rio, proceeded to Malta where she collected two smaller tank landing craft and towed them to Mozambique through the Suez canal. On her way home, whilst refuelling in Aden, the tug was instructed to pick up a Chinese steamer, disabled and drifting in the Red Sea. She was delivered to Aden but it was four years before the salvage claim was settled.

Meanwhile on the Humber the system was continued of keeping two tugs in the river between tides. Known as 'jetty boats' they gave a very useful service to vessels such as trawlers which arrived unscheduled. Up-river towage was falling off as more and more barges became powered and were able to tow other barges, though London barges were being built once more and were gathered up from various yards to be towed in two's and three's to the Thames. The vessels using the town docks (Humber Dock, Princes Dock and Railway Dock) handled a lot of near continental trade but they were generally too small to require a tug. New trawlers and small craft, including tugs, were however fitted out in Princes and Railway Docks and this gave some work to the smaller tugs. The numbers of fishing vessels began to increase as the local trawler companies reconstructed their fleets after the ravages of war and a useful source of revenue to United Towing was established once again. Crews were discharged as they returned from the fishing grounds and tugs moved them around the docks as required and of course frequently brought off trawlers which stranded on the ever-shifting sand and mud banks of the Humber.

The work books show that all the tugs capable of going to sea were actively engaged. The British Iron and Steel Corporation were keeping all their ship-breaking yards very busy and tugs were employed towing a variety of now-redundant military craft, to their final resting place. Concrete barges intended to be sunk as breakwater foundations were disposed of to civilian buyers. *Seaman*, *Superman* and *Englishman* towed a great many of these in pairs to Iceland. Yet more landing craft were going across to the continent, Bilbao and Gijon in northern Spain, and the Baltic ports of Sketin and Gdansk were

Airman and **Krooman** in King George Dock, Hull.

Rifleman.

Serviceman.

35

Masterman (bt. 1941).

Merchantman.

Tradesman (1944).

regular destinations for *Seaman*, *Rifleman*, *Airman* and *Guardsman*. In October 1947 *Merchantman* towed a bucket dredger *Empire Conjuror* from Bombay to Instanbul and in the following month the company commenced what was up to that time its largest single tow, from Rangoon to Buenos Aires. The contract was entered into by three businessmen, an Argentinian, a German and a Briton who had sold the dredger to the Argentinian Ministry of Public Works. Shortly after leaving Rangoon, however, the stability of the vessel was in some doubt, so she was taken into Colombo, whilst the top tumbler was taken off and secured on deck. At Durban the tug's boiler was cleaned and after refuelling at Capetown arrived at Buenos Aires with just 28 tons of fuel remaining! The two craft had departed from Rangoon on 13 November 1947 and arrived at their destination on 21 February 1948, and in the complete round trip back to Hull the tug steamed 24,000 miles, equivalent to once around the world! Prior to this the *Tradesman* had towed the *Thorpe Bay* loaded with canisters of poison gas from Barry dock to a position in the Atlantic south west of Ireland where the steamer and her lethal cargo were scuttled. Whilst on passage with the *Margo* from the Tyne to Wales to pick up another load of canisters the *Tradesman* was relieved by *Seaman* and ordered to Rangoon for the epic voyage recounted above.

Mr. Spink was still the company chairman, and port brokerage and management was controlled by Mr. Vertican. An office at the lock head of King George Dock and another at Alexandra Dock were staffed by a broker at each tide from four hours before high water until work on the tide was finished and each tugmaster had received his orders. Brokerage for coastal towage was also handled by the port department and most of the quotations for ocean tows were done by Mr. Spink, whilst William Cranswick handled the final contracts. The Deck Superintendent was Captain William Cowperthwaite and Mr. Robert Holmes was still in harness as Engineer Superintendent. These early post-war years were a busy time for all departments, an average of twenty to thirty tows being contracted each month in 1948 and some of these tows required two or even three tugs. All sorts of vessels were towed over from Germany as war reparations and quite a lot of steamers were simply scrapped on arrival. In June 1948, *Englishman Tradesman* and *Masterman* towed the battleship *Queen Elizabeth* from off Portsmouth to Loch Striven near Rothesay and the next month *Englishman* took a floating dock from Granton to Torshavn in the Faroes. *Masterman* took charge of an Italian war wreck *Marco Foscarini* from Tripoli to Barrow-in-Furness. She had been loaded with trucks and fuel when bombed by British aircraft and everything had fused in the intense heat of the blaze before she sank. After being raised she was patched up but not surprisingly gave a lot of trouble and had to be taken into Gibraltar and Cobh before reaching England. In August 1948 *Englishman*, *Masterman* and *Seaman* towed the battleship *Renown* from Devonport to Faslane and immediately followed this with the battle ship *Valiant* taken from Devonport to Cairnryan.

The volume of work generated on the south coast by the naval dockyards of Devonport and Portsmouth persuaded the company to put a tug on station at Falmouth or Dartmouth ready for immediate action. *Englishman* was used to tow a number of cruisers to the breakers, the first two being the *Caledon* and the *Delhi*, and *Merchantman* towed the *Draco* to Spain. This Ellerman Wilson vessel had been sunk at Tobruk and after being re-floated was delivered to Valencia. The cruiser *Frobisher* was towed in May 1949 from Devonport to Newport, by *Seaman* and *Superman* and the submarine *Varangian* from Londonderry to the Tyne by *Guardsman* which then returned to Northern Ireland for another submarine destined for the Tyne. Earlier in the year *Tradesman* towed a crane pontoon from Suez to Mombasa and April saw another three tugs in the Indian ocean. *Englishman* towed a British Indian Steamer *Bajora* from Bombay to the Tyne and *Masterman* took another

British India vessel *Varsova* from Bombay to Rosyth.

Masterman left Hull in August to assist the Denmark-Greenland passenger vessel *Julius Thomsen* which was picked up north of the Shetlands and towed to Copenhagen. Tugs more used to river work received the occasional salvage job outside the Humber, and *Krooman*, *Brahman*, *Yorkshireman* and *Airman* combined to help the tanker *Borren Hill*, stranded on the Sherringham Shoal. Brought into the Humber, she was eventually delivered by *Tradesman* and *Airman* to the Tees. During September the ss *Roslin Castle* stranded at Skitterness and the operation to re-float her though crowned with success involved no less than ten tugs. At the end of the year *Tradesman* after taking a tanker barge from Hull to Port Said then picked up the Eagle Oil tanker *San Zotico* and towed her to Milford Haven.

Early in the new year the Shell tanker *Clam* being brought from Reykjavik by the *Englishman* broke adrift in a storm. She drove ashore and some of the crew were lost whilst trying to leave the vessel. The amount of naval traffic was slackening a little, but still provided a number of useful contracts. In May 1950 *Merchantman* and *Tradesman* collected two corvettes each at Montreal for delivery to Germany and the *Airman* had three successive voyages towing submarines from Londonderry to various breakers yards in the United Kingdom. *Tradesman* after towing two hopper barges from the Clyde to Trinidad then collected HMS *Moorpout*, the last British naval vessel in the Bermuda dockyard, for delivery to Devonport. Autumn provided its usual crop of casualties on the Humber and in October and November out of eleven disabled or stranded vessels seven of them were trawlers. Early in 1951 *Merchantman* towed a landing craft from Trincomalee (Sri Lanka) to Harwich. The *Tradesman* towed a similar craft from Singapore to Harwich and *Masterman* connected with a Royal Navy salvage vessel which she took from Colombo to Portsmouth. Nearer home, three redundant whale catchers were brought from Larvik, Norway, for delivery to various breakers yards on the east coast. A welcome

sign of normality after the years of post-war austerity was the return of *Yorkshireman* to Bridlington for her summer season of pleasure trips. She was usually withdrawn from her normal harbour towage duties in April to prepare her for passengers.

A number of ocean tows are recorded for the Spring and Summer including the B.P. tanker *British Sovereign*, brought from Bombay to Newport by *Merchantman*. *Tradesman* towed an Elder Dempster coaster *Knowlton* from Lagos to Milford Haven. Two stowaways made their appearance soon after the tug left Dakar and since there was no run crew on the tow they had to be taken off by lifeboat from the *Tradesman*. Also from west Africa, this time Freetown (Sierra Leone), *Englishman* brought the coaling hulk *Faraday* which was delivered to Newport. In July 1951 *Masterman* towed two corvettes from Baltimore to Kiel and the next month *Merchantman* collected a floating dock at Southampton. She was delivered to Belem de Para at the mouth of the Amazon and was destined for the Peruvian port of Iquitos some 2000 miles up river. The *Englishman* (Capt. Tim Bond) and *Merchantman* (Capt. Bill Hopper) took the British India passenger vessel *Khandalla* from Gravesend to the Clyde. They were relieved by local tugs off Greenock on the 23 December and told to remain there over the Christmas period and maintain radio watch. On the 27 December they were instructed to proceed to Campbel-town, familiar to Capt. Bond from his period in command of rescue tugs there during the war. Here they stayed on salvage station until midday 29 December when they steamed south after being informed of a number of casualties in the south west approaches, including an American cargo-passenger vessel the *Flying Enterprise* which was to become a considerable celebrity at the time. The US transport *General Greenly* and USS *Southland* responded to her distress call and rescued the passengers and crew. Her master, Capt. Carlsen, insisted however, on remaining aboard to try and save his ship. The m.t. *Turmoil* arrived on the scene and her mate Kenneth Dancy leapt aboard to assist the captain in

Guardsman.

Superman (1933).

Krooman.

Handyman.

making a connection. The tow commenced in deteriorating weather and as the strong south-westerly winds were driving her towards the English Channel it was decided to take her to Falmouth and avoid the coast of France. Before the contract to tow *Flying Enterprise*, the *Turmoil* had already taken the Shell tanker *Mactra* in hand after she had lost her rudder whilst steaming in ballast.

Capt. Hopper of the *Merchantman* gave the followig account of the events:-

"The *Merchantman* hugged the Irish Coast to avoid the heavy seas on the way south. Our only radio equipment was wireless telegraphy and almost all the distress traffic was being worked by radio telephone. This put us at a great disadvantage as we could not get any information from vessels or coast stations but eventually we were both ordered to Falmouth at 1900 hrs on 1 January 1952 and anchored alongside of the *Englishman* which was already there and anchored. Whilst I was rounding Lands End and the Lizard that evening we had passed the *Turmoil* with the *Mactra* in tow and running before a westerly gale. Shortly after we passed her the *Turmoil* broke away from her tow. She eventually reconnected and handed her tow to local tugs in Falmouth on 2nd January. *Turmoil* had a partial crew change etc, in Falmouth bay, and it was there her new mate Kenneth Dancy joined her. Late on 2 January the *Turmoil* left Falmouth to assist the *Flying Enterprise*. We on the *Englishman* and *Merchantman* felt very much we should have had the job, because without a crew on board the *Flying Enterprise*, the chances of getting a good connection were very remote, especially in the weather conditions prevailing. Without radio telephony also we were very much in the dark as to what was happening".

The *Flying Enterprise* with a split in her hull was taking in water and listing as she was slowly towed towards the south coast by *Turmoil*. She became the focus for the world press who soon filled all the available hotel space in Falmouth. On Monday 7 January the *Englishman* was chartered by the Associated Press and steamed with a posse of reporters and photographers in search of the stricken vessel now the centre of a considerable flotilla of craft. The *John W. Weeks*, a destroyer, had passed over supplies of food to Capt. Carlsen and the Trinity House tender *Alert* along with numerous other vessels had been chartered by hungry news-hounds.

Capt. Hopper takes up the story again:-

"Wednesday 9 January, we in the *Merchantman* were chartered by Associated Press. The reporters covered most of the British dailies. After getting the reporters on board we sailed from Falmouth at 11 am. I was having the greatest difficulty in finding the position of the *Flying Enterprise*. Nobody would answer our call for information, and we couldn't get any information from the *Englishman* because they were constantly transmitting radio messages for the press. After leaving the Lizard, I was steering for a position based on press reports, but after about an hour we managed to get a direction radio bearing on the *Englishman's* transmission. By the time I reached the flotilla the afternoon was beginning to dull. Various crafts were signalling me to keep clear but I carried on to get close to the vessel. It was too dull for the photographers, but they sighted her and made their reports. I then had to go to the *Englishman* and get some packages of film and reporters papers and then set off back for Falmouth. The weather was not too bad, the wind about west-south-west, force six. The *Flying Enterprise* was laid beam to the sea and laid well over on her port side. It was very evident that she would sink within 24 hours, but Capt. Carlsen and mate Dancy were still on board".

The tow in fact parted at 1.30 pm. on 9 January only sixty miles from Falmouth and it proved impossible to reconnect. *Merchantman* anchored in Falmouth at 11.30 pm that day, but with reports that the *Flying Enterprise* was still afloat, Capt. Hopper received another charter this time from the newsreel companies *Paramount, Gaumont British* and *Movietone*. All were determined to film the last moments of the sinking vessel and embarked at 9 am loaded with their cumbersome equipment. The weather worsened and *Merchantman* arrived on the scene with most of the camera crews seasick and very sorry for themselves just as Capt. Carlsen and Dancy, mate of the *Turmoil*, were being taken off. *Turmoil* had engaged her tow under Lloyds 'open form' so the loss of *Flying Enterprise* meant that for all the endeavours of her master and crew, and especially the heroic efforts of the mate, it was a case of 'No cure — no pay'.

Captain Hopper:

"As soon as the rescue was completed I moved in close to the *Flying Enterprise* to give the camera crews their opportunity to get good pictures. One cameraman had his equipment wrecked before he got any film taken. The vessel rolled him and his camera right hard on to a bulkhead so I put the deck crew to look after the remaining camera crews. I steamed within feet of the lifting bow as she lay starboard side up. The seas were rolling over her and our camera crews took the only moving pictures of the whole episode. At 4 pm her bow lifted up in the sea and she slid stern first down to the bottom".

She went down 11 January 1952, about forty-five miles off the Lizard in a strong gale force westerly wind, force 7 to 8, and it was another rough passage home for the *Merchantman* which arrived back in Falmouth at 11.30 pm much to the relief of the camermen. On the afternoon of 12 January, two days later, Capt. Hopper was busy again on stand-by as a fire-fighting vessel after the cargo of the *City of Lichfield* ignited. Several years later as master of the *Tradesman* he had another encounter with *Turmoil*. In June 1954 he took a relief master out to her five hundred miles west of Lands End where he brought off Capt. Parker to be at the bedside of his daughter who was dangerously ill. Latterly in Greek hands the *Turmoil* went to the breakers in May 1986.

CHAPTER FOUR

RUNNING OUT OF STEAM

The British Steel Corporation (Salvage) Ltd. continued an active programme at their breakers' yards giving regular work to United Towing vessels. *Tradesman* towed a tug and dredger from Lisbon to Dar-es-Salaam in February 1952 and then proceeded from Mombasa to the Firth of Forth with a Royal Navy lifting vessel. There was the usual crop of stranded trawlers dealt with by the harbour tugs and *Merchantman* towed a fractionating column from London to an oil refinery then under construction at Swansea.

On 31 October, *Englishman*, steamed out of Singapore bound for Blyth towing an obsolete tanker, *Olcades*. Trouble began at Suez with delays in obtaining clearance through the canal, then whilst in the Mediterranean off Malta the tow was lost. During the night with the wind refreshening from the north the master of the crew of 'runners' decided he would ease out the anchor cable to which the tug had its towing gear connected. Unfortunately he did this without informing the tug and consequently the brake would not hold and the chain ran out so fast it broke its last link to the chain locker. The cable was cut loose as it was quite impossible for the tug to recover her gear with the power available and the *Masterman* was despatched from Hull with replacement towing gear. A rendezvous was made off Gibraltar from where the tow was resumed, but off Cape Roca the master's cabin lamp rolled off the table causing a fire which completely destroyed the bridge. *Masterman* had fortunately remained in company and the run crew went aboard her whilst the tow was taken into Lisbon. Eventually the *Englishman* proceeded on the homeward voyage as far as Flamborough Head only to be engulfed in one of the worst storms ever recorded for the seas around the British Isles. During the beginning of the new year of 1953, coronation year, the Thames and east coast were devasted by floods, a ferry foundered in the Irish sea and numerous ships were driven ashore or sunk in the fury of the wind and water. *Prizeman* was also parted from her tow which was recovered by *Merchantman*, whilst *Brahman* towed in the Spurn light vessel which had dragged about eight miles off station. A mountainous wave struck *Englishman* and *Olcades* and the cable parted. The bosun was lost overboard and a seaman smashed against the engine room casing suffered a broken leg and several damaged ribs. The master headed the tug for the Humber with the tow rope trailing and once in the shelter of the estuary the line was recovered and the injured men sent ashore. As the captain brought the gear aboard it had to be man-handled along the deck; wet, the four hundred yards of chain cable, 20 inch manila and thick wire ropes weighed about four tons, but waterlogged this was just about doubled and it would have been quite impossible to accomplish the task out in the open sea. *Englishman* was diverted to assist the *City of Dundee* (Hall Line) disabled by engine trouble off Flamborough head and escorted her safely into the Humber before going in search of her missing charge. The tanker came to rest on the shore near Yarmouth more than seven miles from where they had parted. It took two months to refloat her and she was eventually delivered by *Englishman* to the breaker's yard at Blyth in mid-April.

Tradesman towed two hopper barges from Hull to Port Said, and in April 1953 *Englishman*, *Tradesman* and *Seaman* combined to haul the aircraft carrier *Formidable* from Portsmouth to Inverkeithing.

Merchantman towed a tanker from Maracaibo to Barry and the *Tradesman* after taking two more hopper barges to Port Said, then towed the Khedival mail steamer *Al Rawdah* from Alexandria to Rosyth. In August and September 1953, *Tradesman*, *Masterman* and *Rifleman* each towed two trawlers from Bremerhaven to Boston, Mass., though the *Rifleman* had to make a stop at the Azores to refuel. United Towing often had the task of picking up redundant tankers or other cargo vessels laid up in Cornwall where the extensive waters of the Fal estuary provided an ideal berth. There was usually a full day's work of preparation before the tow was ready for sea; a steam line had to be rigged up from the tug, often across the deck of another vessel, and the towing connection made ready for passing down. Navigation lights were set up and the run crew with all their bedding, provisions, stores etc. had all to be taken aboard before finally getting under way. Working from early morning it was usually nightfall before the roadstead was cleared and the sea gear could be streamed.

The last vessel to be built at Gateshead, the steamer *Galeon*, was returned there in January 1954 by *Tradesman* from the port of Gothenburg to be broken up. *Airman* towed two motor hopper barges from Port Said to Rotterdam, and then in August *Tradesman* was occupied with two twin screw motor river ferries, named *Khalid* and *Sher Afghan* which were towed from Nantes, to Chalna, East Pakistan. At the same time a contract was made to convey four ferries from the Firth of Forth at Granton to Marmagae in Portuguese India by the *Masterman*, *Merchantman*, *Rifleman* and *Guardsman*. These craft were converted landing craft and during the voyage out *Merchantman's* tow *Bonny Prince Charlie* developed serious structural defects and it was decided to take her into Cherbourg.

Tradesman reached the Indian ocean during early September coinciding with the south west monsoon which was blowing very hard. Her charge had already been repaired after structural faults became evident and the two ferries suffered more damage which necessitated putting back to Aden for further attention., Here they joined *Masterman*, *Guardsman* and *Rifleman* to await the end of the monsoon before continuing their journey in early October, and the *Glenfinnan*, *Flora MacDonald* and *Eriskay* were eventually delivered to India. It was January of 1955 before work on *Bonny Prince Charlie* was completed and *Merchantman* continued her tow, and

then in the spring took the steamer *Eastway* from Bombay to Hong Kong whilst *Airman* towed a small motor vessel from Lagos to Hull. At home there were lots of coastal tows and *Englishman* hauled the monitor *Abercrombie* from Portsmouth to Barrow-in-Furness. During a storm in March 1955, the Norwegian passenger liner *Venus* drove onto the rocks at Plymouth Sand and *Englishman* and several navy tugs successfully refloated her. *Tradesman* after keeping salvage station at El Ferrol sailed for Casablanca and towed the French motor vessel *Safi* to St. Nazaire before escorting *Venus* from Plymouth to Ijmuiden. *Tradesman* was constantly at work and sailed from the Tyne with two B.P. oil exploration landing craft, *Gimada* and *Geboso* bound for Port Moresby. They departed on 18th August and arrived in New Guinea on 12th November with refuelling stops at Port Said, Aden and Djakarta. The tow covered a distance of 11,309 miles, the company's longest to date, at an average speed of 5.86 knots.

On the way home she collected a tank landing craft from Benghazi on Christmas day to delivery to Malta and then towed the Port Line vessel *Port Fairy* from Piraeus to Palermo. There were the usual trawler casualties on the Humber during the Autumn, four vessels being assisted during October after going aground. Contracts for handling naval craft were still being rescued and in November 1955 the aircraft carrier *Campania* was towed by *Englishman* and *Merchantman* from Sheerness to Blyth and *Englishman* took the cruiser *Argonaut* from Portsmouth to Newport. At the end of the year the motor tanker *Royal Crown* was picked up by *Englishman* and *Merchantman* and towed to Falmouth, the second time she had received assistance from United vessels.

The new year began with some long ocean tows. *Masterman* took a store ship from Doha (Qatar) to Bombay, and *Tradesman* left the Tyne towing another B.P. landing craft to Port Moresby after delivering the Federal line vessel *Kent* from London to Blyth, with the assistance of *Masterman*. In June, *Tradesman* left New

Welshman, *formerly the naval tug* *Growler*.

Foreman, *first sea-going motor tug.*

Autocrat towing the Hull-New Holland ferry pontoon.

Fenman towing **Rudolf** of Gothenburg.

Marksman.

Guinea to have her boilers cleaned at Mombasa before continuing to Zanzibar from where she towed the steamer *Al Said* to Hong Kong after bunkering at Colombo. The *Al Said* was the personal yacht of the Sultan of Zanzibar which he used when visiting the isle of Pemba or mainland Africa. From Hong Kong *Tradesman* proceeded to Djakarta to pick up a landing craft which was delivered back to Hong Kong. Her next task was to tow an ex-Japanese passenger vessel from Djakarta, but twenty miles from Hong Kong the latter sank and was a total loss. In the Spring, *Airman* and *Rifleman* each towed a steamer from London to Piraeus, and *Merchantman*, after taking a tanker from south west Ireland to Liverpool, towed a landing craft from Cardiff to Montreal. *Englishman* delivered a motor vessel from Grangemouth to Quebec and towed a suction dredger from Buenaventura to Balboa. She followed this by towing a steamer from Callao to Milford Haven. *Merchantman* took a steamer in charge at Montevideo in October 1956 and hauled her to La Spezia. Whilst at Colombo in the following month, *Tradesman* received news of the tanker *Drafn* aground at Minicoy island on her maiden voyage. Despite having driven ashore at a speed of 14 knots she was refloated at the first attempt which gained a salvage award of £21,958. *Tradesman* steamed on towards Aden when information was received through the British warship HMS *Cheviot* that a German vessel *Max Arlt* (only built in 1955) had grounded on a reef on the east side of the Male Atolls (Maldive Islands). The navy had taken off the passengers but could not remain in the area to assist further. After three tides and many difficulties *Tradesman* managed to refloat the distressed vessel and escorted her into the anchorage at Male. Another substantial award, £16,500, was received for this operation and the tug steamed on to Aden to pick up the steamer *Velho* destined for Hong Kong. At Colombo the first mate of the *Tradesman* was left ill in hospital and she finally arrived in Hong Kong on 11th February 1957 after a refuelling stop at Singapore. She was the only United Towing vessel out east at the onset of the Suez crisis in the previous October which resulted in a temporary closure of the Canal and a reversion to the long route around the Cape. During March *Tradesman* towed a Shell Oil tank landing craft from Hong Kong to Miri, Borneo, and then steamed to Labuan to pick up a coastal barge for pulling to Hong Kong. After surveys and refitting she proceeded to Djakarta with a Shell bunkering barge and after some engine repairs she sailed home through the Suez Canal which was now declared open to traffic. *Tradesman* returned to Hull in July 1957 after eighteen months absence during which she had steamed 56,000 miles, the equivalent of more than twice around the world, 30,551 miles with a tow; of 364 days at sea, practically all were in the tropics.

At the beginning of the year five trawlers received assistance in the Humber and *Merchantman* towed a landing craft from Phillipville, Algeria, to Dakar. There was still plenty of coastal work and in April *Merchantman* towed a new motor vessel from Grangemouth to Montreal. *Rifleman* took a barge and crane pontoon from Rotterdam to Port Harcourt, Nigeria in September and *Englishman* towed a tanker into Falmouth after breaking down in the south western approaches. United Towing were beginning to feel the impact of overseas competition chiefly from the Dutch fleets of Smit Internationale and Wijsmuller, but also from Bugsier and Unterweser in Germany. Most of their rivals were extensively equipped with modern diesel vessels, fitted with a towing winch which greatly aids a tug when entering or leaving harbour. The winch can automatically shorten or lengthen the tow line reducing the strain and likelihood of the cable parting. When towing off a hook the lengths of rope and wire are fixed and can only be varied if weather and tidal conditions are suitable. The United Towing fleet, though large and versatile enough to handle all manner of tasks, was increasingly underpowered and in need of new vessels to replace a collection of vessels either built pre-war or in the 1940's. In fact none of them were of more recent build than 1946, though they were otherwise well-found craft manned by excellent crew. The *Englishman* (ex-*Enchanter*, 1943) can be taken as an example of the peak of steam tug development and even the earliest motor tugs tended to follow closely the form of this design. Competitors with diesel craft were able to keep down their costs to much lower levels and increase profitability. Firemen were not required which saved three men's wages while the use of a towing winch reduced deck manning and cut down on the delays resulting from heavy weather. In England, Overseas Towing and Salvage operated with a fleet of three tugs, the largest of which was the Admiralty tug *Turmoil* on long-term charter. Built during the latter years of the Second World War as one of a class of ocean rescue tugs, she frequently maintained a salvage station in the south western approaches in direct contention with United Towing. As recounted in the previous chapter she had taken on tow the *Flying Enterprise* which the skippers of *Merchantman* and *Englishman* thought they should have had. As another of the same class of tug was available from the Admiralty it was contemplated taking it on 'bare-boat' charter to meet the Overseas challenge.

During October 1957 twenty-one contract tows were completed, six were obsolete destroyers or frigates being taken for demolition, one was a Greek steamer picked up in the North Sea after running short of fuel and there were trawlers in varying degrees of distress. In the same month *Masterman* and *Tradesman* arrived at Quebec with a mark VII landing craft in tow from Liverpool across the Atlantic. *Tradesman* then hauled an oil exploration craft from the Tyne to Dar-es-Salaam and *Masterman* was engaged in the Mediterranean. Homeward bound from east Africa in January 1958 *Tradesman* met up with a loaded oil tanker *Esso London* in Bitter Lake, Suez Canal, for towing to Bari in Italy. The tanker had a damaged rudder and propeller after running into the canal bank during a dense fog. A Dutch tug *Witte Zee* of Smit International assisted in the operation and after discharging her cargo in Bari the *Esso London* was towed

out to sea to clean her tanks, after which she was taken to Toronto for laying up. Ever busy, *Tradesman* then proceeded to Malta and towed a submarine to the breakers at Gateshead. *Masterman* also towed a submarine to the Tyne and *Rifleman* was similarly engaged when caught by a storm in the Bay of Biscay. The tow rope parted and after fruitless searches lasting nearly a week, it was presumed her tow had sunk. However two Spanish fishing vessels encountered the submarine about a month later. She was taken into the Spanish port of Pasajes and the fishermen laid a salvage claim.

In April 1958 it was finally decided to take a five year charter on one of the ocean tugs available from the Admiralty. She was the *Growler*, built in 1943, and renamed *Welshman*. Her first job the next month was in company with *Englishman* to take the battleship *Howe* from Devonport to Inverkeithing for demolition. *Welshman* then took a fleet tanker from Devonport to Rosyth, and the cruiser *Liverpool* from Portsmouth to Bo'ness. Most of the sea-going fleet was kept occupied with coastwise tows and obsolete warships, bought for scrap by the British Iron and Steel Corporation, were a prominent feature of this work. *Airman* undertook the movement of yet another landing craft which she picked up in Yugoslavia and delivered to Surabaya in Indonesia. She was followed by *Merchantman* with an identical task after towing a salvage vessel from Ardrossan to Ceuta. Early next year *Merchantman* took a work platform from Emden to Kharg island in the Persian Gulf. *Englishman* embarked from Hull in March to connect with a Ben Line vessel at Smiths Knoll where she was found lying at her sea anchors after breaking down, and conveyed her to Teesside for repairs. Whilst on salvage station *Englishman* assisted a Dutch coaster with her engine room flooded during heavy weather. She was towed to Falmouth and pumped out by the tug, which then went to the aid of a Norwegian tanker in the Bay of Biscay and escorted her to Brest. *Englishman* also picked up a Swedish vessel loaded with fruit off the Channel Islands

Waterman.

Headman.

Larkspur, acquired from Fosters, remained in service until 1962.

Lancelot and *Acetut*.

and took her to Southampton. Prior to this good run of salvage work the stalwart *Englishman* had already towed the cruiser *Boxer* fronm Devonport to Barrow-in-Furness and the cruiser *Cleopatra* to Newport. *Welshman* undertook a long ocean tow in September 1959 conveying the obsolete US aircraft carrier *Shamrock Bay* from Boston, Mass., to Hong Kong and then delivered an obsolete tanker from Bombay to Kure in Japan. *Masterman* escorted a dredger from St. Michael's in the Azores to Nassau in the Bahamas, and *Englishman* and *Seaman* towed the cruiser *Cumberland* from Devonport to Newport. In December *Englishman* engaged the 1563 ton Norwegian tanker *Landbreeze* and towed her into Falmouth after which they continued to the little Swedish port of Skutskar in the Gulf of Bothnia where she was intended to supply power for a timber mill during the winter months.

Englishman towed a tanker from Gothenburg to Blyth in spring 1960 and then assisted *Merchantman* and *Seaman* caught in a storm with another tanker off the coast of Norway. After safely bringing their charge to the Tyne, *Englishman* steamed to the English Channel to connect with a jack-up work platform. She was then in the hands of an American tug with low fuel capacity and not enough horsepower to move her expeditiously to Kharg island in the Gulf. In June *Englishman* towed a vessel which served as a tanker for a fleet of whalers from Sandefjord to Blyth and another similar vessel from Southend to Inverkeithing. Then followed a tanker taken from Falmouth to Faslane and a Harrison Line vessel from Liverpool to Ghent. During September she towed five British tankers from Falmouth and Portland to Cardiff and refloated the Everard vessel *Antiquity* stranded off the landing berth at Dean Quarry, inshore of the Manacle rocks, Cornwall.

On the evening of 10th September 1960 the 7659 ton *Indian Merchant* collided with the *Baron Herries* (Kelvin Shippng Co.) almost cutting her in two at the foredeck. The Penlee lifeboat which was new and as yet unamed stood by until the arrival of *Englishman* which led the crippled vessel in thick fog to safe anchorage in Falmouth. *Baron Herries* turned out to be so badly damaged that her owners decided to sell her for scrap. The lifeboat, later christened by Lady Tedder as the *Solomon Brown*, was herself lost with all hands when assisting the *Union Star* in 1981. In October *Englishman* was laid alongside the Empire Wharf at Falmouth, keeping salvage station, when during a freak squall the big Admiralty floating dock broke from her moorings. She bore down on the tug which had her motor lifeboat hung from the davits but resting on the water. The lifeboat was crushed to matchwood and the *Englishman* suffered damage to her hull which was later repaired, and she just managed to steam ahead to avoid being pushed right through the jetty. As a finale for the year, *Englishman* salvaged a Danish vessel located in a severe storm, held fast with her sea anchors, and eventually towed her to Southampton.

Already in 1959 the start of vital changes in the composition of the fleet had taken place, presaging a rebuilding programme not seen since pre-war days. In May United Towing took delivery of their first sea-going motor tug *Foreman*, built at Beverley by Cook, Welton and Gemmell. Fitted with a Ruston Hornsby eight cylinder engine developing 1030 b.h.p., she maintained the appearance of a steam tug however by having a dummy funnel and the engine exhaust led up the main mast. Another significant change in the old order was the death of T. C. Spinks on 7 November 1960 who at the age of 84 was working in his office. He had been managing director for forty years since the formation of United Towing in 1920. Appropriately after his unswerving devotion to the company his ashes were scattered at sea off Spurn point from the deck of the tug *Yorkshireman*. Shortly after Mr. H. Vertican, himself with many years of experience, was appointed as the new managing director. Back in 1954 United Towing had completed the purchase of the Foster tug fleet, but this was still operated as an independent company though with a senior broker transferred to the Foster offices to co-ordinate the activities of the two fleets. In 1960 Foster's was finally merged with United Towing and over the next three years their seven tugs were sold for scrap. The newest was the *Tidspur* of 1943 and the oldest *Acetut* originally built for the Hull Barnsley Railway in 1886.

Welshman towed another obsolete aircraft carrier from Boston, Mass., to Hong Kong in June 1960 and yet another of the same from Balboa (Panama) to Japan in November. *Englishman* was contracted to guide a loaded Swedish oil tanker *Polyana* (15980 tons) from off Port Said to a terminal at the Isle of Grain. She had suffered an explosion in which the bridge had been destroyed and could be steered only from below deck. Some of *Englishman's* crew went aboard the tanker to assist her own small complement and she was discharged at the Isle of Grain before being towed to Gothenburg. Early in 1962 *Masterman* connected with a steamer which had lost her propeller in the North Sea and took her to the Tyne for repairs. After completing her tow to Japan, *Welshman* returned to the United States and brought a Danish motor vessel from Jacksonville, Florida for delivery at Hamburg.

A further move towards the introduction of diesel power took place when *Serviceman* was converted from steam and fitted with a six cylinder British Polar engine developing 1575 b.h.p. Equipped with a towing winch she was recommissioned in October 1961 and her first task was to bring into the Humber a trawler with disabled steering from a position eight miles north east of Withernsea. *Airman* towed two new tugs from Germany to Istanbul, and *Masterman* two passenger ferries from Glasgow to the same destination. *Merchantman* picked up a twin screw motor vessel off the Algerian coast and towed her to Palermo and then after towing a crane barge to Aden, she delivered a Japanese motor vessel from Mauritius to Singapore. During the summer *Welshman* was diverted to the Gulf of St. Lawrence to take over a large lake steamer which had proved too much for *Tradesman* to handle. A day out from her destination at Genoa, Tim Bond, master of the *Welshman* and one of

the most experienced tug masters in the country died in his cabin. He had served as tug master of the ocean rescue tug *Bustler* during the war and with his many active years in the company was regarded as United Towing's commodore. The navigating officer brought *Tradesman* home to a sad return.

Welshman was still very active and in December towed a drilling rig for BP from the Tyne to the Gulf. During her passage through the Bay of Biscay severe weather damaged the legs of the rig which was taken into Gibraltar for remedial work before proceeding through the Mediterranean. This was only the second jack-up drilling rig United Towing had been involved with and it turned out to be a harbinger of things to come as will be related in a later chapter. *Welshman* followed this tow with a large dredger taken from Kuwait to Suez. Numbers of dredgers, harbour construction pontoons and the like were taken to Israel at this time by *Rifleman*. This was a sensitive period in the Middle East and any craft known to have used an Israeli port was prohibited entry by the various Arab nations. Certainly at Suez log books were always asked for and studied closely and this automatically barred any vessel which had contact with Israel from transit through the Canal.

CHAPTER FIVE

A NEW BEGINNING

The modernisation, begun in 1959, which had seemed so desirable made little progress and the result was that early in 1962 United Towing was experiencing serious financial difficulties. Fortunately, the company's potential was recognised by Basil Parkes, chairman of the Boston Deep Sea Fishing group, who negotiated the purchase of United Towing and initiated a programme of development to prepare it for a vigorous new era of expansion. The *Englishman*, now nearly twenty years old, was sold to Portuguese owners, who renamed her *Cintra* and several of the smaller harbour tugs were put up for sale. During 1961 *Roman* and *Overgarth* had already gone for scrap, and in 1962 the ancient *Acetut*, *Lancelot*, *Merman*, *Linesman* and *Larkspur* were all sold and towed to Rotterdam by United tugs. Three small diesel river tugs were brought from London, the *Brentonian*, *Jaycee* and *Scorcher*, respectively named *Bargeman*, *Lighterman* and *Keelman*. All were powered by six cylinder Lister Blackstone engines, developing 324 b.h.p., and were the first craft in United's fleet to have controls for the main engines on the bridge. Basil Parkes, now the Chairman of United Towing, and at the time Sheriff of Hull, also started a rebuilding programme, the first radical replacement campaign since before the war. Two twin screw diesel tugs to be named *Headman* and *Workman* were ordered from Cochranes of Selby. Intended basically as harbour tugs they were capable of short coastal tows with a speed of 11 knots and a rating of 1320 b.h.p. Four smaller tugs, *Trawlerman*, *Tidesman*, *Tugman* and *Motorman* were built by Humber St. Andrews on the fishdock slip-way and delivered over a two year period from February 1963 to February 1965. *Brahman* and *Headman* were both sold in 1962 to U.K. owners and the *Merchantman* went to Italy where she was registered at Naples as the *Tarentum*. *Tollman* capsized early that year when acting as stern tug assisting a vessel out of Alexandra dock. The tug's engineer and a deck boy were drowned, but the vessel was later raised and put back into service. This accident resulted in a critical look at the towing-hook system and it was decided that all new units would be fitted with the 'Seebeck' type of tow hook attached to a radial arm travelling 180° on a track. In the event of a full broadside pull the strain would be directed away from the centre line and would tend to lift the tug rather than drag it over. The hook was also fitted with a release mechanism which could be activated by a pull wire from the bridge. It was further decided that this system would be gradually installed in all the vessels of the existing fleet.

During the summer of 1962 *Rifleman*, *Airman* and *Serviceman* all had tows which took them to the new Israeli port of Ashdod and because of the Arab embargo on nations trading with Israel were therefore ruled out of any voyage which involved transiting the Suez Canal. In September, *Welshman* after escorting a vessel from Montreal to Piombino in Italy went through the Canal to pick up a vessel destined for Rotterdam. Work for the scrap industry was falling off but there were still a few coastal tows to be found and *Welshman* came in useful for the heavier jobs. Trawler casualties continued to give revenue as they had for the last forty years especially during the Autumn and early part of the new year. *Irishman* was sold to Italian owners at Cagliari in Sardinia where she was renamed *Genaggentu*, and another tug was ordered for port work, this time from Drypool Engineering of Hull. *Riverman* with a single variable pitch screw and Bronz engine of 900 b.h.p. was delivered in January 1963. The country was experiencing the most severe winter conditions since 1947 and ice had to be broken before she could be shifted from her fitting-out berth in Princes Dock. More of the old steam tugs were being towed away for scrap. *Salvage* and *Bowman* were taken to Rotterdam by *Rifleman*; *Cockspur* and

Fenman to Maasluis by *Foreman*, and *Yeoman* and *Tidspur* to Hendrik Ido Ambacht, also in charge of *Foreman*. The *Serviceman* at this time was the company's most economical unit and was handling tankers and other large vessels on coastal tows, but *Welshman* because of her large crew was proving too expensive and could not compete, so she was taken off salvage station and tied up in Victoria dock. In February *Trawlerman* entered the fleet and both *Headman* and *Workman*, delivered from Cochranes in April, were soon busy with coastwise tows. They towed on the hook rather than with a winch and proved very manoeuvrable with their twin eight cylinder Lister Blackstone engines. *Tidesman* was completed in June 1963 and joined *Trawlerman* her sister ship. The twin-screw vessels had bridge control and a fuel capacity of thirty-nine tons.

Another improvement was the installation of V.H.F. radio with communication to a control station at head office manned by the brokers. Eventually they were connected through to their homes and the ease with which orders and instructions could be transmitted made a dockside presence unnecessary. The lobby at Alexandra dock was therefore demolished and the one at King George dock rented out. Three more London river tugs were purchased, *Stamford Brook*, *Tyburn Brook*, *Colne Brook*, which were renamed *Dockman*, *Pressman* and *Patrolman* respectively. Larger than the first three they also had more power and it was decided to build new bulwarks all round to increase safety for the crew when working in the Humber. They had been designed originally for running under the stem and stern of barges and operating in relatively sheltered waters. Constructed at Henry Scarrs, Hessle Shipyard, each was furnished with a seven cylinder British Polar engine of 520 b.h.p. *Boatman* and *Waterman* were sold to D. Cook of Hull and it was decided not to renew the charter of *Welshman* which was returned to the naval dockyard at Devonport. During the entire year there were no long distance overseas tows and with the exception of a dredger taken from Nantes to Leghorn it was all coastal work. The Hull trawler fleet began selling a lot of obsolete vessels and tugs were kept busy delivering them to breakers both within the U.K. and on the continent. An important change in the company hierarchy took place in June with the retirement of Mr. H. Vertican after a lifetime in the towing industry. The managership was taken over by Mr. Tony Wilbraham to provide progressive new leadership in this vital period of restructuring.

The *Krooman* sank at her berth in King George dock and it was the end of August two months later before she was raised. Capitalising on this unfortunate accident it was decided to strip out her steam engine and convert her to diesel. Drypool Engineering fitted a twelve cylinder Bronz engine but it was January 1965 before the resurrected tug entered service again. At the end of 1963 the last of the old ocean tugs, *Tradesman*, had been sold to Greek owners who renamed her *Vernicos Kitty*. Three tugs were ordered from Charles D. Holmes (Beverley) each 230 tons gross, with two six cylinder Allen engines of 2000 b.h.p. Furnished with towing winches holding 200 fathoms of wire they were slightly under 100 feet long with two screws and twin rudders. *Tradesman* was the first to be completed in July 1964 followed by *Merchantman* and *Masterman* in the Autumn. *Masterman* had the same dimensions as the other two but was provided with twin eight cylinder Lister Blackstone engines of 1320 b.h.p. Instead of a conventional towing winch she had a winch with large warping drums and was also different by having one lifeboat whereas the *Merchantman* and *Tradesman* each had two. *Tugman* was also delivered from Humber St. Andrews in September. The company had no large ocean tugs now and so coastal tows were the staple, but leavened by the occasional salvage job. In the summer *Workman* towed *Lady Sybil* and *Lady Jean*, two of J. H. Piggot's tugs, from Grimsby to Inverkeithing for scrapping. *Seaman* and *Pinky* were themselves taken to Queensborough for demolition and *Superman* towed *Biddy* to the same destination where both remained for breaking up. The Grimsby tug company J. H. Piggot and Son was taken over by Basil

Salvage c.1960.

Tidesman.

Riverman.

Headman.

Dockman.

Parkes, but still retained its separate identity as a company though management was now a joint operation with the United headquarters at Hull.

At the end of 1964 no less than ten trawlers were assisted in the Humber estuary and its approaches, and 1965 began with the delivery of the *Motorman* last of the tugs ordered from Humber St. Andrews. Again there was plenty of activity towing away redundant trawlers to the scrapyard but the old established system of maintaining jetty tugs between tides was abandoned because of the high wage bill it entailed. Whenever possible a coastal tug on a voyage agreement maintained station on one of the river jetties. The Spring of 1965 was important as the start of a fruitful involvement with the offshore oil and gas industry. After completing an exploration well for Shell (UK) Exploration and Production, the drilling rig *Mister Cap* was ready to be moved to another site. United were the only company in the United Kingdom able to meet the demand for the type of tugs required and in the first week of April *Masterman*, *Merchantman* and *Tradesman* connected with the three-legged jack-up drilling barge (complete with helicopter landing pad) in the northern section of Dogger Bank and hauled her thirty miles further south. *Guardsman* was chartered to act as a supply vessel along with *Hector Gannet*, a small stern fishing trawler of 361 tons as the area was out of the helicopter's range and a rig supply vessel was not available at the time. The tow rails and other gear had been removed from *Guardsman* to give a clear afterdeck. Sunderland was established as the base port but the journey proved a severe ordeal for the rig crews who more often than not arrived at their destination too sea-sick to leave the tug by the rig crane and personnel basket. During these operations *Hector Gannet* was holed when she hit one of the legs of the *Mister Cap* and was herself towed to Sunderland by *Guardsman*! Also in April *Merchantman* was contracted to meet the self-propelled drilling ship *Glomar IV* in the south western approaches and assist as needed until she arrived off Great Yarmouth. Early next month *Merchantman* and

Tradesman assisted the construction crane ship *Global Adventurer*, whose task was to erect and pile steel jackets to form the base for drilling or accommodation modules. *Merchantman* was equipped to lift and run out the huge mooring anchors, then the two vessels collected a series of barges from Rotterdam carrying the steel jackets which were lifted or skidded off alongside the *Global Adventurer*. The first location was close to the Indefatigable bank to build an exploration unit for Conoco. Some damage was inevitable because of the nature of the work but heavy fendering for close contact work reduced this to an acceptable level and the tugs success lead to many lucrative deals with the offshore industry. The next rig to appear was the *Endeavour*, a tilt-leg jack-up platform, which was to be located off Hartlepool. The legs were hinged outside the hull and before reaching the drilling site they were given a seven degree spread. United tugs positioned this rig for the first time in late May 1965 and before the month was out, *Englishman*, *Serviceman* and *Masterman* towed the B.P. rig *Sea Gem* from a work platform at Middlesbrough, where she had been built, to an anchorage some thirty five miles off Spurn point.

Each time a rig was moved a deck superintendent had to go out and board her to co-ordinate the manoeuvres of the tugs. There were no brokers involved at this time and tugs were ordered very much on a personal basis and at very short notice. Every move involved at least three coastal tugs and a tug would also be employed to run passengers, perhaps with provisions and small items of equipment, to and from the rig.

After being towed to a new site near the Owers and Leman bank, *Mister Cap* developed structural problems with the leg guides caused by the nature of the sea bed. She was jacked up on a sand bank and the scouring effect of the tide exposed the bottom of the legs and rendered her unstable. Eventually it was decided that her construction was unsuitable for the North Sea and she was towed to the coast of Nigeria. To replace her Shell chartered *Neptune I*, a French drilling rig which was also taken in hand by United Towing. During the summer, *Englishman* was sent to Cuba to pick up the 11,149 ton *Athelcrown* which was brought to Hull on her first ocean tow, and in August the *Yorkshireman* familiar to so many summer visitors at Bridlington was taken to Boom, near Antwerp, for scrap. *Serviceman* was contracted to tow a vessel from mid-Atlantic to Funchal, Madeira, and then hauled a dredger from Falmouth to a position off Cape Finisterre. At Christmas 1965 BP had ordered six tugs to move *Sea Gem* to a new drill site but just as they were getting ready to depart, the news came that whilst preparing the rig for the move the jacking system had failed and the structure collapsed. There was heavy loss of life and some of the tugs were later hired to take out equipment for the salvage operation and act as wreck markers to warn shipping of the danger of entanglement with the huge construction.

The new year began with a contract for *Englishman*, *Headman* and *Workman* to proceed to Middlesbrough and collect *Ocean Prince*, the first semi-submersible rig to operate in the north Sea. An easterly gale warning had been issued and against the advice of the tug masters and towing superintendent the rig controller insisted on sailing. The next day when the gale struck, the rig was forced to anchor and a further three tugs were ordered from Hull to ensure her safety. Meantime the vessel marking out the location broke down, and she was towed into the Tyne by *Rifleman*.

Eventually *Ocean Prince* was towed into place some twenty miles off Flamborough in the face of strong easterlies and snow showers.

Rig-moving became a part of life and later in the year two of Piggot's tugs *Lady Alma* and *Lady Cecilia* were frequently used. It was realised that to meet the off-shore challenge successfully new and more versatile craft must be built. Four twin screw tugs, 97 feet overall and 2400 b.h.p. were ordered from C. D. Holmes at the Beverley shipyard. They could serve as harbour tugs if needed. Two larger vessels were ordered from Cochranes at Selby. Also twin screw they were 128 feet overall with

engines developing 3220 b.h.p. *Norman* reappeared in the fleet in February after conversion to diesel, and *Waterman*, intended for upriver work and dock work with smaller vessels, was delivered from Richard Dunstons yard at Thorne. Only 57 feet she was a twin-screw craft with two six cylinder Bergius-Kelvin engines at 420 b.h.p. During April, *Rifleman* towed *Tollman*, *Handyman* and *Lady Thelma* to the breakers at Bo'ness. In May the company acquired *Universal Star* a small stern fishing trawler, to be converted for charter as a general purpose North Sea tender able to run stores, crew and divers to rigs or construction craft. The A-frame was removed and the fish room made into accommodation for a diving team. She was peculiar in that although a twin-screw vessel the two engines were of different sizes. The port engine had six cylinders, and the starboard four, which meant that a careful check on fuel and water consumption had to be kept otherwise she developed a list to port. After only two years she was sold to Offshore Ltd. and United purchased another fishing vessel, the drifter *Dauntless Star*, in October 1966 which was operated with a run crew of five as a stand-by vessel with various drilling rigs. She required no modification other than using the fish room for stores and galley coal, and the spanker boom was adapted to lift the lifeboat which was housed athwart the stern. In February she was sold to Aberdeen and returned to fishing, The rig *Orient Explorer* was brought out of Rotterdam in May to drill off the Leman bank for Shell Exploration, but after only two bores she was taken into Europort for modifications during October. *Neptune I* whilst engaged off Ravenscar in July developed a leg can collapse and was towed into Bridlington Bay before she also went to Rotterdam for repairs. *Englishman* brought the new rig *Transocean* out from the Tees assisted by *Hermes*, a tug belonging to the Swedish Neptune Salvage company, but temporarily under United management. In all, during the year the company handled 26 rig moves quite apart from contracts for crane barge work and towing barges with components. *Welshman* was delivered in November and

Merchantman.

Englishman.

Norman.

Seaman.

65

Irishman.

Yorkshireman.

after a few days on display in London was soon put to work. A twin screw tug of 451 tons gross she developed 3220 b.h.p. and was fitted with a double drum towing winch. She was followed in January 1967 by *Seaman* from C. D. Holmes yard at Beverley and *Irishman* (sister tug to *Welshman*) from Cochranes. The *Seaman* was the first of a class of four tugs later fitted with a special winch to handle the anchors of construction crane barges and pipe-laying barges. A little under a hundred feet overall and 261 tons gross, the two Ruston Hornsby six cylinder engines drove twin screws and developed 2400 b.h.p. which rendered them capable of a static pull of 25.5 tons.

In 1967 there were three crane barges at work and United was involved with them all through arrangements made with Brown and Root (UK) Ltd., the main contractor for construction work in the North Sea, with bases at Great Yarmouth and Rotterdam. A couple of American tugs complete with crews were brought over to work jointly with the United tugs. *Neptune I*, damaged in the previous year, was not returned on station until September 1967 when *Lady Alma* was the only tug available. As a result the Swedish tug *Carl* was taken on charter but her fuel capacity only just allowed her to reach the destination. The old steam tugs *Forto* and *Presto* were bought from the Ellerman Wilson line but laid up the following spring and towed to Blyth for scrap in June 1968 whilst demands of the offshore work resulted in modifications to various elements of the United Towing fleet. *Seaman* was fitted with an anchor winch and her stern modified with a roller system for lifting anchors. The propellers and rudders were protected by a tubular grill to prevent fouling and some heavy fendering was provided at the stern. *Superman* and *Yorkshireman*, delivered from C. D. Holmes in April and June respectively, were similarly treated and *Hullman*, still under construction, was altered before delivery. In June 1967 *Welshman* and *Irishman* brought *Transocean I* out of Bremerhaven and in doing so created a local controversy. The rig had a German crew and they wanted German tugs to have the job, but the American area manager had been impressed with United's handling of *Transocean I*, her sister rig, and insisted on using the company's tugs again. *Hermes* was kept busy and used on ordinary commercial tows as well as for offshore contracts. *Irishman*, *Serviceman* and *Headman* collected *Neptune I* from the North Sea and took her into Dunkirk for maintenance work before she was moved to drill in Italian waters. Another rig, *Mister Louie*, was blessed with twelve cylindrical legs and a very slow jacking speed which made her very vulnerable to foul weather when being moved.

During September 1967 *Irishman*, *Welshman* and *Merchantman* were contracted to move the semi-submersible rig *Ocean Prince*. While the three tugs were making their connections, *Merchantman* ran too far astern and was pierced by one of the longitudinal pontoons. Taking water rapidly, she managed to get alongside a supply boat and the crew abandoned ship shortly before she sank. The *Staflo* another semi-submersible and with a draft of about thirty-five feet about the biggest unit in the North Sea at the time, was brought out of the builder's yard on the Tees in December. She was successfully located about seventy miles east of Aberdeen on the 14th of the month ready to start boring a well for Shell Exploration. *Irishman* sailed from Hull to Cobh to berth the supertanker *Olympic Champion* (37744 tons) on 25 December because none of the local tugs either at Cobh or Milford Haven would work on Christmas Day. Soon after *Seaman* and *Superman* went over to Rotterdam to tow the crane barge *Atlas* to Bantry Bay to assist in the construction of the oil tanker berths for the new refinery being built for Gulf Oil. During the entire year the company's tugs were involved with no less than thirty-seven rig moves with additional contracts towing crane and construction craft.

Englishman left Hull on 11 November to connect with a pipe layer and trench barge, designated M228, at Rotterdam which was towed to Kuwait by the Cape route. She then took a tanker from Bahrain to Hong Kong, a dredger from Hong Kong to South Vietnam and assisted in refloating a tanker aground on the coast of Sumatra. Finally *Englishman* hauled a loaded tanker from Cape Town to the Thames which, after discharging, she towed to Rotterdam before arriving back in Hull on 24 October 1968.

New production platforms for gas were being built for B.P. about thirty-five miles off the Humber estuary and tugs were frequently required to run both personnel and equipment to the construction sites. On 15 January the semi-submersible rig *Sea Queen* broke from its moorings during a severe gale and *Irishman*, *Seaman*, *Serviceman* and *Masterman* were asked to assist. The rig was brought under control and moved to a temporary location near Flamborough Head before towing to Rotterdam for modifications. Because of the heavy demand on United's resources the Immingham tugs *Lady Cecilia* and *Lady Alma* were frequently called on to help in rig moves. They with *Headman* and the Dutch tug *Gröningen* brought out the new rig *Sedneth II* from Rotterdam for Shell Exploration. The fleet had been enhanced by *Hullman* delivered from C. D. Holmes in March and immediately contracted for anchor work. After the free-wheeling early days in the offshore business bureaucracy began to make itself felt. Customs collectors had decided that the continental shelf was equivalent to a foreign port and excise formalities had to be gone through every time a tug sailed or arrived back at Hull. Tug brokers however were still not very evident and most of the requests for tugs came direct from the clients. The tally of rig moves for 1968 was forty-one including the *Neptune Gascoigne* towed from Bordeaux to Djerba (Tunisia) by *Welshman* and *Irishman*.

CHAPTER SIX

THE ADVENT OF THE SUPER TUG

During 1968 the oil and gas industry provided an enormous amount of work and the company's tugs ended the year with a total of forty-one rig moves to their credit. The dangers inherent in offshore drilling were emphasised by the loss of the *Ocean Prince* which broke up and foundered on the Dogger Bank. In January 1969 United Towing took over the management of the *E. Bronson Ingram* recently completed at Cochrane's Yard for the Ingram group of America. Registered in Panama this twin screw tug, powered by two Ruston Hornsby engines developing 5000 b.h.p., proved a very useful tug for rig work. Her first job was to assist with the *Gulf Tide*, then in the spring she took the crane barge PM 24 from Rotterdam to Ortona, Italy, where her owners finally took command.

The company realised that to satisfy contemporary needs larger and more powerful tugs were required. Closure of the Suez Canal had resulted in the construction of a generation of huge tankers, an economy of scale necessary when using the Cape route. The supertanker and the existence of large semi-submersible rigs demanded a new breed of tug. United Towing decided to invest in the building of a 'supertug' to enable them to meet the challenge. The design was entrusted to Burness, Collett and Partners, and a model of the proposed vessel was tank-tested on the Isle of Wight, but it was to be another two years before the *Lloydsman* entered service. In the meantime an American owned, Liberian registered tug *Alice L. Moran*, was acquired to provide the company with the necessary 'muscle' for the heavy, long distance tows. Built in Japan in 1966 she was 189 feet overall, 1,167 tons gross with four General Motors engines driving twin screws. The four sixteen cylinder units, two on each shaft, developed 9.600 b.h.p. and towing was from an electric double drum. Renamed *Statesman I* she was collected from New York on 15 August and sent to Madeira on station until work was found for her. Meanwhile the crew had time to get to know her unfamiliar equipment and sailing characteristics.

In September *Englishman* and *Irishman* commenced the tow of *Ocean Traveller*, a semi-submersible rig from Stavanger to the Cape of Good Hope. Off Walvis Bay *Englishman* developed rudder trouble and so *Statesman I* was despatched to take her place. At home the *Hullman*, while assisting a tanker, *Conoco Arrow*, to come off the oil jetty on 28 November, was overrun as the crew were recovering the towing hawser. The mate and two seamen were drowned as the tug foundered but she was raised soon after and put into dry dock on 9 December. After leaving *Ocean Traveller*, *Irishman* was sent to Luanda to collect two barges for delivery in Rotterdam. She picked up a small vessel with an engine failure on the way and towed her into Luanda. Meanwhile *Statesman I* and *Englishman* with her rudder problems sorted out were in Durban awaiting further orders when they received instructions to assist the Shell super-tanker *Mactra* after an explosion in the Mozambique Channel. Shell also engaged *Seaman*, *Superman*, *Masterman* and a Dutch tug, *Mississippi* to move the drilling rig *Staflo*. Shortly after they commenced to recover the anchors, strong south easterly gales developed which persisted for almost four weeks and the move of only thirty-five miles was not completed until the end of January 1970. Forty-two rig moves had been undertaken throughout the year and the anchor-handling tugs had assisted in offshore operations as far afield as Nigeria.

At the beginning of the new year, *Irishman* and *Welshman* were contracted to tow the rig *Louisiana* from Luanda to Las Palmas, and in February *Statesman I* picked up the *Kollbryn*, (51396 tons), another tanker casualty in the Mozambique Channel, which she took into Durban. The company had appreciated the value of stationing vessels in the Cape area with the increase of traffic caused by the canal closure and a relief system was arranged for the crews. In home waters rig moves continued to keep tugs busy and explorations began to move into the higher latitudes off Shetlands. During April 1970 *Seaman* and *Superman* towed *Berkshire*, a newly completed vessel strike-bound at Sunderland to Hamburg to be fitted with special steel hatch covers. Also in spring *Yorkshireman* towed the Royal Sovereign Light Tower out from Newhaven where the concret base unit and an accommodation module had been built in an excavation on the beach. After completion a channel was cut for the base unit to be floated and hauled out to Newhaven Pier where she was ballasted down until *Yorkshireman* took her in tow. *Masterman* was also on duty and took two pontoons for placing in the excavation basin before the entrance channel was filled in again. The pontoons served as the float-out base for the light tower and accommodation block, and early in June *Welshman* towed the main caisson of the light tower from Newhaven Pier to its permanent location at the Royal Sovereign shoals off Beachy Head. *Workman* assisted while the caisson was ballasted down to the seabed on top of the base unit and *Welshman* then proceeded to Portsmouth to pick up a large floating crane to take to Naples. An Elder Dempster vessel arriving in June from West Africa with a cargo of mahogany logs grounded whilst attempting to enter King George Dock. After discharging some of her cargo into lighters she was refloated the next day through the combined efforts of seven tugs. It was only this year that a separate salvage department was established under the control of a salvage superintendent, but unfortunately loss of the log books for 1970 leave the record of the company's progress during the year somewhat sparse. Early in December a collision took place near the Dowsing light vessel and the bow of the *City of Liverpool* penetrated the engine room of the *Jark*. She made water rapidly, but *Foreman* took her in tow and *Foreman* arrived with a pump so that the *Jark* was safely brought into dry dock at

Immingham for repairs.

At the start of 1971 the *E. Bronson Ingram* was again temporarily placed under the management of United Towing who supplied her crew while operating from the Gulf of Mexico. In March off the coast of Brazil her master died and was buried at sea and the tug later put in to Trinidad where the owners relieved the United Towing crew. *Welshman*, *Irishman* and *Yorkshireman* together towed the rig *Staflo* from the Firth of Forth for relocation, but had to seek temporary shelter in the Moray Firth when caught by a south easterly gale. Intense competition for offshore work meant that now most orders were placed by brokers acting for the owners of the rigs and it was important to have sea tugs on stand-by awaiting instructions. *Headman* remained on station at the Ekofisk oil production platforms in all weathers to assist tankers loading oil at the mono-buoy, but was also called in to help with the Royal Sovereign light tower. The light tower superstructure, consisting of platform, accommodation block, engine room, lantern and helicopter landing pad supported on its building piles, stood complete and ready to be moved in February 1970. The ground was excavated from beneath the platform to where the two pontoons had been positioned the previous season. From there the trench was continued to the sea allowing the tide to run in and float the pontoons between the supporting piles and under the platform. *Headman* having the least draught was used to pull the unit out and clear of the beach so that *Tradesman* could connect with the bow of the pontoons. These critical operations depended on the spring tides, coupled with fine weather, and by 9 am the next morning the Royal Sovereign tower was moored securely in Portsmouth harbour until the final stage of the operation was to take place. On the 11 May *Hullman* and *Lady Cecilia* commenced a tow of sixty-six miles to the Royal Sovereign shoals but after nine hours a bad weather forecast was received and they returned to Portsmouth. On Saturday 15 May with a promise of fine weather the tow began again and at noon on the following day the

Statesman I *towing tanker buoy* ***Brent Spar****.*

Lloydsman towing the *Venpet*.

tower was in position over the main caisson at high tide.

The operation was completed in a smooth sea when as the tide went down the tower settled onto the caisson and the pontoons were pulled away. After returning to Newhaven the latter were finally towed to Rotterdam by *Lady Cecilia*.

During February 1971 *Statesman* was sent to Freemantle to connect with the jack-up rig *Jubilee* which she towed to Singapore before taking a new semi-submersible rig from Japan to the Cape. On the 16th February *Lloydsman* was launched at the Leith shipyard of Robb Caledon Shipbuilders. Slightly over 250 feet long she was the most sophisticated craft yet to have entered the United Towing fleet. The two main engines were coupled through a reduction gearbox to a single screw with variable pitch set in a 'Towmaster' nozzle. There were two towing winches one capable of a 100 ton pull, the other of half that, with closed circuit TV cameras giving the bridge a clear picture of activities on deck. Facilities included a comprehensive workshop and excellent radio and radio telephony equipment. The crew of twenty-four officers and men lived in fully air-conditioned quarters with access to laundry, drying room and hospital. After extensive trials culminating in her bollard pull at Europort she returned to Hull and was ready for service on 4 October. A fortnight later she was chartered to move the semi-submersible rig *Neptune 7* in the northern area of the North Sea, but the operation was delayed by bad weather. Another semi-submersible rig had in the meantime developed serious structural problems and the towing superintendent was air-lifted by helicopter from *Neptune 7* to TW61 which had to be towed into sheltered water as quickly as possible. *Lloydsman* made a successful connection and pulled her into the Firth of Forth. On 23 October *Hullman* retrieved an anchor of derrick barge PM24, but was caught by the tide and collided heavily with a sharp corner of her hull. Making water rapidly she very soon sank but not before all the crew had reached safety. This was the second time *Hullman* had gone down but this time no effort was made to salvage her. In November and December three rigs were moved including the *Sea Quest*, taken from the Firth of Forth to Flushing. *Irishman*, *Welshman* and *Seaman* brought her to a temporary location off the Humber in the new year and in mid-March she was towed to a new drilling station in the northern sector of the North Sea. *Englishman* connected with the tanker *Mobil Libya* (48908 tons) during February and after a week long tow they arrived off Durban. The next month *Tradesman* took *Miranda* acting as tender to the United Kingdom trawler fleets in northern waters from Iceland to Leith. The jack-up rigs *Orion*, *Sedneth II* and *Britannia* were taken in hand as were a number of semi-submersibles.

The fleet was enhanced with the purchase of the West German tug *Bremen* on 4 April 1972, whilst at Durban. Built at Bremerhaven in 1967 she was 166 feet long and 1182 tons, with two engines geared to a single shaft. The propeller operated in a nozzle and the eight cylinder diesels generated 5340 b.h.p. Most unusually she towed directly through a hawse pipe in the stern bulwarks. Immediately put to work under her new name *Euroman*, she picked up a crane barge for delivery to Capetown, but receiving a salvage call relinquished her tow and proceeded to the assistance of a tanker on fire near the coast. The blaze was put out and the cargo of oil transferred to another while anchored in Mossel Bay, before the ravaged vessel was towed into deep water and scuttled. *Euroman* then returned to Port Elizabeth picked up the crane barge and completed her tow to Capetown, before being sent off to Mombasa to assist a vessel to Karachi.

On the Humber in late May a Ben Line vessel grounded on top of her anchor making an approach to King George Dock but was successfully refloated. The next month *Statesman* towed a materials barge from Rotterdam to Houston and *Lloydsman* went to South Africa to keep salvage station. On passage she picked up a tanker abandoned after a fire and took her into Gibraltar, where the cargo was transferred before

Euroman.

Scotsman.

Yorkshireman free running.

hauling her to Rotterdam, an operation which began on 16 July and was completed on 5 October. *Statesman*, after delivering her tow to Houston, refuelled at Freeport, Bahamas, and then proceeded to Cabinda, Angola. Here in September she picked up the rig TW58 for transporting to the North Sea, but towards the end of October when off the Canaries handed over the tow and headed for home. On passage *Statesman* was diverted to pick up a cattle ship which had broken down mid-Atlantic after sailing out of the Saint Lawrence for Europe. She was towed to her anchorage at Grosse Island near Quebec and the tug then went into Sydney, Nova Scotia, for some engine repairs before finally returning to Hull on 17 December. *Englishman* had sailed for Montreal in August where she picked up a loaded materials barge for delivery to Hudson Bay. She returned to Newfoundland with a barge, and whilst berthing her *Englishman* sustained damage to her rudder and propeller, needing attention on a slipway at Buri Peninsular before she could proceed. A loaded materials barge was towed down the west coast of Newfoundland and after discharge taken to Halifax, Nova Scotia. Here *Englishman* remained on station for a while before heading back across the Atlantic to arrive in Hull on 7 December. *Euroman* still on call off the South African coast left Durban early in November to assist a disabled tanker, the *Gallant Colocotronis* (28917 tons) in the Mozambique channel. She was hauled into Capetown on 3 December, but within an hour of arriving *Euroman* was answering another distress call. This time the casualty sank and the tug returned to Durban empty-handed.

At the end of 1972 the company had only three tugs working, *Statesman*, *Seaman* and *Yorkshireman* which were all engaged to shift the rig *Ocean Viking*. Between March and November six tugs had been disposed of, *Scotsman*, *Prizeman* and *Norman*, all pre-war vessels converted to diesel power, were sold to Drapers of Hull for demolition, and the others found new owners. *Pressman* went to London, *Patrolman* was bought by a Greek company and *Foreman* by Kings of Bristol. A United Towing crew took her to Avonmouth and on the way towed a coaster into Plymouth with a complete engine failure.

CHAPTER SEVEN

COD WARS, RIGS and CHARTER HIRE

1973 started in routine fashion with *Lloydsman* back at Leith for repairs to her propeller nozzles and *Irishman* undergoing modifications to equip her for anchor-handling from the stern. For work with rigs in the North Sea *Euroman* was contracted to tow a Brazilian tanker from Dubai to Germany by the Cape route. She commenced her voyage on 25 January 1973, but developed engine trouble and was replaced by *Welshman* and *Scotsman*. The latter was formerly the *E. Bronson Ingram* which after being placed under United Towing management on more than one occasion, as we have recounted before, was eventually purchased from her American owners on 27 February whilst lying at Amsterdam. The two vessels connected with a tanker which had suffered fire damage after being in collision and could only be hauled with safety stern first.

The events occuring off the coast of Iceland at the time were, however, far from routine and after the imposition of the fifty mile limit by the Icelandic Government British trawlers attempting to fish closer inshore were being harassed and threatened with arrest. This was the second of the so-called Cod Wars which had broken out first of all in 1958 with the unilateral declaration of a twelve mile limit, and had been rekindled in 1971 with a further extension to fifty miles. To prevent any serious and possibly fatal encounters with an Icelandic patrol vessel the Ministry of Agriculture and Fisheries chartered *Statesman* to act as a buffer tug whose job it was to try to get between the gunboat and any hard-pressed trawlers. On 12 February *Englishman* was also chartered by the Ministry to join *Statesman* which by this time had switched from Liberian to British registration to avoid any diplomatic complications which might result from her new role. General harassment of the trawling fleet continued up to the first week in April when there was a major incident involving the gunboat *Aegir*. *Englishman* intervened after she had cut the trawl warps of the *Ross Resolution*, *Kingston Emerald* and *Saint Keverne*, and the Icelandic vessel responded by firing four shots across her bows, two blank and two live. A few days later another gunboat *Odinn* cut the warps of *Saint Dominic*, and a West German trawler, then *Wyre Victory* and *Primella* were on the receiving end when *Thor* entered the fray. When *Englishman* appeared soon after this latest incident the commander of the gunboat fired a blank shot and threatened to sink her. As the Cod War intensified the British government decided to hire a third tug of the United Fleet to increase protection for the fishermen in Icelandic waters. The vessel chosen was *Lloydsman*, then the world's biggest, fastest and most powerful tug, and she was ordered back from Dubai on 22 April as soon as she had completed towing the rig *Isle de France* from Port Noire, Gabon. The reaction from the gunboats was to cut the warps of the *Aldershot* and *Kestrel* and the captain of the *Thor* threatened to open fire on the *Statesman*. A fourth tug, *Irishman* was chartered at the end of April and at the same time it was announced that talks were to be held in Reykjavik so long as there were no further acts of aggression against the fishing vessels.

It had been agreed with the Ministry of Agriculture and Fisheries that the tugs patrolled for a month at a time and then went into port for a day to take on fuel, reprovision and change the crew. *Englishman* used Lerwick, Shetland, as harbour but *Statesman* and *Lloydsman* returned to Greenock. Peace was short-lived, however, and the gunboat *Thor* with her 40 mm cannon manned and sharp shooters armed with rifles on deck tried to cut through the trawl wires of the *Crystal Palace*. When *Englishman* and *Irishman* intervened she opened fire with blanks, then early in June, during further dangerous manoeuvrings, *Odinn* collided with *Lloydsman*. On 20 July *Welshman* relieved *Irishman* which returned to Hull for repairs and along with *Yorkshireman* and

Scotsman then served as tug and anchor-handler for the derrick barge *Hercules*. At the end of September *Englishman* was taken off the Icelandic patrol and came to Hull for dry-docking. Finally on 16 November *Lloydsman*, *Statesman* and *Welshman* all arrived in Hull after a temporary settlement had been arranged between the contending nations.

While these extraordinary events were occurring in the waters off Iceland the rest of the company's vessels were engaged in the more usual activities expected of a modern fleet of tugs. *Welshman* towed the crane barge *Big R* from Corunna to Hull where she arrived on the 5 March. She was to be used to provide the piling for the foundations of the M62 motorway where it crossed the Ouse. *Scotsman*, *Superman* and *Yorkshireman* brought the rig TW58 from Rotterdam to a North Sea location. A very heavy tow, this particular rig had a structure called a 'mat' covering the base of all the legs which generated a great deal of underwater drag. In early May *Masterman* was engaged to run anchors and tend on the drill ship *Wimpey Sea Lab*. Starting life as the *Elizabeth Bowater* the converted vessel was now drill-coring off the Northumberland coast searching for an underwater coal seam on behalf of the National Coal Board. *Yorkshireman* towed the trawler *Huddersfield Town* from Faroes to Grimsby, and *Tradesman* followed the same route with the *Ross Khartoum*. The rig *Ocean Viking* was moved in mid-June and late next month *Euroman* was available for work again after extensive engine repairs in Rotterdam. Along with *Superman* she engaged with the rig *Orion*.

Another new addition to the fleet had been made on 7 June with the purchase of *Jaramac 28*, renamed the *Norman*. Formerly the *Frederick B. Ingram* she was built by Cochranes in 1968 as the sister ship to the *E. Bronson Ingram*, which had already been acquired and renamed *Scotsman*. A twin-screw vessel with two eight cylinder engines developing 5000 b.h.p. she underwent extensive refitting before entering service on 8 December. The bridge was modified, a new anchor winch installed and extensive work was carried out in the engine room and on

deck. Throughout the late summer and autumn all of the fleet except those chartered by the Ministry were engaged in rig moves or towing construction craft. *Seaman* set out in November with two small dredging craft from Brest to Cuba with refuelling stops in the Azores and Bermuda. *Masterman* assisted the liquified gas and chemical carrier *Fernwave* after a fire at sea and brought *Kingston Pearl* off Burcom Sand, where she had been beached for temporary repairs after being holed in a collision, and towed her to Grimsby. At the end of the year *Statesman* was put into dry dock at Immingham to be fitted with controlled pitch propellers.

The formation of Star Offshore Services in 1974 was an attempt to create an organisation easily identifiable to the potential customer in need of the assistance of tugs for offshore contracts. In a joint venture with Blue Star line a supply vessel was purchased and *Irishman*, *Welshman*, *Scotsman* and *Norman* were made available to the new company. They were in demand mainly for anchor-handling with derrick barges and pipe-laying vessels, and were generally occupied on a longer period of charter hire compared with the short term arrangements for rig moves. Along with Blue Star Technical Management a design was put on the drawing board for an anchor-handling craft with a bollard pull of 90 tons. After tank tests and considerable research and development, four tugs of this class were ordered from Dutch Shipyards. Two of the tugs were to be owned directly by United Towing and two by Star Offshore, though it was not until 1976 that they were finally delivered.

The year had opened with only one tug working outside of the North Sea. She was the *Euroman* which after leaving Cuba arrived in Hull on 21 January. In the same month *Englishman*, after taking on fuel at Immingham oil terminal, was swept by a strong ebb tide into the jetty. A vessel of Humber Tugs trying to give assistance was also brought up against the jetty and *Englishman* had to be dry-docked at Immingham for repairs after which she sailed to San Pierre, off Newfoundland, to pick up a tow. Early in February

Salvageman *alongside the big tow.*

Yorkshireman towing the C. S. **Monarch**.

Scotsman.

Riverman was taken to new owners at Haugesund in Norway, and *Yorkshireman* was transferred to Humber Tugs and renamed *Lady Theresa*. *Lloydsman* was back in commission after a lengthy refit and *Statesman* was given trials after the installation of her new controlled pitch propellers. She did her bollard pull at Rosyth early in March after being inspected at Aberdeen. Soon after *Statesman* was involved in a salvage bid for the *Oregis* which had run aground on the Tyne after losing power. An inflatable rubber boat launched in order to establish a connection unfortunately capsized in the surf and a young seaman was drowned. Shell Exploration took *Statesman* on a long charter to work mainly with rigs in northern waters. In October Shell Exploration and Production sent her to Halifax, Nova Scotia, to pick up the rig *Stadrill* for towing to Europe. Many problems ensued and *Statesman* had to put into Newfoundland before proceeding to Dundee where her charter ended.

Irishman was engaged as an anchor-handling tug at the Ekofisk complex working with derrick barge M26, and during the Spring and Summer *Masterman* was contracted to assist the Canadian cable ship *John Cabot* working in the western approaches. She served as general hand-maiden, holding the cable ship steady into the weather when required and tending to her diving team. In July *Masterman* was transferred from Ocean Tugs to Humber Tugs.

Throughout the year the whole of the sea-going fleet was fully occupied except for dry-docking and repairs. The U.S. construction company, Brown and Root, had United Tugs working with their crane barge or towing materials barges and the salvage department was having a lifting craft built at Penryn, Cornwall. This led to United getting a contract to tow a floating cargo ramp under construction at the same yard. *Lady Vera* towed it to the Thames for a paper manufacturing company.

During September *Euroman* and *Lloydsman* were both in the same dry dock at Wallsend undergoing surveys. Then *Lloydsman* sailed from Clydebank on 20 October with a new jack-up drilling rig *Key Victoria* to Cabinda, Angola, where she arrived on 17 November. From here she moved *Stormdrill VII* arriving off Lagos, Nigeria on 23 December. On the same day *Welshman*, whilst sheltering from a storm at Peterhead, drove onto rocks but was quickly re-floated and put into dry dock at Aberdeen for inspection. *Lloydsman* proceeded to Luanda in January 1975 to collect a Sedco semi-submersible rig and, despite problems caused by the local political situation, departed on 7 February, arriving off the Portuguese coast on 26 April after calling at Las Palmas. She then went into Cadiz for a well earned rest. After dry-docking, surveys, change of crew and replenishment of stores, *Lloydsman* set out for Dakar. On the way she had refuelled at Gibraltar, picked up an engineer at Dakar and finally delivered the jack-up rig *Al Ittihad* to Abu Dhabi, on 25 July. The rig had been delivered to Abu Dhabi by *Euroman* which after refuelling at Dakar proceeded to the Bonny River and sailed on 2 June towing the rig TW59 bound for Trinidad. Meantime at Muscat *Lloydsman* took an Italian tanker in hand and whilst waiting for the delivery of some machinery went to the assistance of another tanker which had broken down, and towed her to an anchorage off Muscat. Departing on 19 August the tanker was delivered at Genoa on 27 September. *Superman* was engaged on a long term charter with Rigging International and operated mainly between Hamburg and the east coast ports of Britain. *Euroman*, back in Europe, towed the Antarctic survey vessel *Discovery* from Tenerife to Barry dock. *Lloydsman* was brought back to the North Sea for winter rig moves, but on 18 November she was once again chartered by the Government to use as a buffer-tug in what proved to be the final phase of the Cod Wars. *Euroman* was brought to Rosyth from where she also sailed to Icelandic waters on charter to the Ministry of Agriculture and Fisheries.

At the same time *Tradesman* and *Lady Theresa* were both chartered by the French company C. J. Doris to tow out to sea a half-mile of ten inch steel pipe supported by air vessels. The pipe was constructed at Evanton air field

Lloydsman.

Serviceman.

Winchman.

84

Linesman.

Guardsman.

on the Cromarty Firth in an experiment to see if pipe-laying could be simplified by joining up long lengths at sea instead of the laborious business of towing and welding a great number of short sections. The end of the pipe whilst on shore was some half a mile from the nearest point the tug could approach, so a wire had to be run out at low tide for the tug to heave on. In all, the operation lasted nearly a month from 18 November to 10 December.

Early in December the *Norman* was returning to the Humber at 5.35 on the morning of the 13th, after a rig move, when she began to take water very rapidly. Six miles north of the BP platforms and about thirty-five miles north east of Spurn, she sank. The crew thankfully were all rescued by the platform stand-by vessel, and it was concluded that *Norman* had sustained undetected damage through contact with the rig she had been towing.

1976 began with *Statesman* going to Iceland to join *Euroman* and *Lloydsman* in trawler protection duties, which meant that the three largest ocean tugs were now on Icelandic patrol. *Seaman* and *Superman* were still on charter to Oceanic, barge-towing, as they had been much of the previous year and *Englishman* and *Lady Vera* were on hire to Rigging International, also for barge-towing duties. *Irishman* and *Scotsman* were serving with Star Offshore Services and on 19 February the first of four new tugs was delivered. Specifically designed for the offshore industry the *Guardsman* was 154 feet long, 885 tons gross with two six cylinder Mirrlees Blackstone engines driving twin-controlled pitch propellers in nozzles. The main engines developed 7,200 b.h.p. giving a maximum speed of 14 knots and there was also a bow thrust engine of 600 hp to improve manoeuvrability. The towing winch had a capacity of 100 tons, and the anchor winch 130 tons. Ten days later *Winchman* was also delivered and was registered in Hull, though the *Guardsman* was put on the London register.

In late March a contract was made to tow TLP, a large concrete structure, down the Firth of Clyde to new moorings at Loch Fyne. *Guardsman* and *Winchman* were employed along with four smaller tugs chartered from Alexandra Towing. The United Towing Superintendent was in charge of the operation which took two days. This huge tow had a draught of 49 metres and a height of nearly four hundred feet. The *Linesman* and *Serviceman* completed the quartet of offshore tugs, and were delivered at Rotterdam in April. The company against keen competition won a contract with RDL at Methil to undertake the float-out of a steel fabricated jacket for Shell. The *Brent A* Structure was enormous with a weight of 15,000 tons, a length of 510 feet and over two hundred feet high. Four tugs were employed, *Scotsman*, *Englishman*, *Seaman* and *Lady Theresa* as well as a supply vessel and a diving team. Over a lengthy period *Brent A* had been gradually jacked across from its construction site to a position on the shore over two materials barges. Designated NS11 and NS12 the latter were situated in two specially constructed basins open to the sea and ballasted down though a system of hydraulic pipes controlled remotely from the shore. When the jacket was positioned correctly the barges were deballasted on the rising tide so that heavy seating trestles would meet up with special saddles attached to the jacket. As the tide rose the jacket was lifted clear of the ground and in suitably calm weather the tow began. It was important that the two barges were towed evenly otherwise they tended to wedge into the basins. The next stage was to pull the combination of barges and jacket, and secure it within four mooring buoys. Ballast was then run into the barges which sank down to the sea bed leaving the *Brent A* structure, made of tubular steel with sealed ends, to float clear to be hauled to a pre-arranged site, where the saddles were jettisoned for recovery later. The final sea tow to the operational site was contracted by a Dutch company who in fact chartered *Guardsman*, *Winchman*, *Linesman* and *Scotsman* from Star Offshore Services. The whole project which began on 5 May was very lucrative for United Towing and her associated company. *Brent A* was floated out on 5 May and separation from the barges was completed two days later. *Englishman*, *Seaman* and *Lady Theresa* looked after the two barges when they were refloated and took them to the Tyne.

The Cod War reached a final settlement in the early summer and on 1 June *Lloydsman* was released from her duties as a buffer tug. She went into Swan Hunters for her five year survey and repairs to damage received in skirmishes with Icelandic gunboats. At the same time a bow thrust was fitted to enhance her agility. *Euroman* and *Statesman* were also released by the Ministry and the latter was employed towing a flare tower from Erfjord to the Brent B location. *Lloydsman* as soon as her refit was completed was employed in rig moving and all the new Star Offshore tugs were on long term charter for construction work. *Irishman* was sold to Guybulk Shipping Ltd. of Bermuda and a United crew delivered her to Georgetown, Guyana, where she was renamed *Kwakwani*. The next month *Euroman* went to the Amphitrite Shipping and Trading Co. of Panama who renamed her *Petrola Ocean Master No. 24*.

After extensive repairs and survey *Superman* left Middlesbrough on 25 November with the Land and Marine barge *Odinn* bound for Montevideo with scheduled stops at the Cape Verde Islands and Rio de Janeiro. The barge was very heavily laden with pipe-pulling equpment, a crane, heavy wire reels, and oil and sewage pipes. *Seaman*, *LadyTheresa* and *Lady Vera* were all on long term charter at Loch Kishorn assisting at the Howard Doris Construction site and *Lloydsman* was at the Swan Hunter yard, Wallsend, undergoing modifications. She was there throughout October and November and departed on 11 December to collect a rig on the Clyde. Built by Marathon the *Al Ghallan* was towed through the Suez Canal to Abu Dhabi.

CHAPTER EIGHT

CRIPPLED TANKERS AND POLLUTION CONTROL

Superman arrived at Rio de Janeiro with *Odinn* on 29 January 1977 after a stop over at the Cape Verde Islands where she was delayed by strong winds. A fortnight later she was at Montevideo and by 25 February the barge was towed to a location off Maldonado. *Lloydsman* arrived at Abu Dhabi on 7 February with the rig *Al Ghallan* and then returned to Europe where at the end of March she was in the Baltic to pick up a new semi-submersible rig, *Atlantic II* for delivery to the Firth of Forth. The end of the following month saw *Lloydsman* at Flushing to tow the jack-up rig *Gulftide* across the Atlantic to Halifax, Nova Scotia, where she collected the semi-submersible rig *Sedco I* bound for a site in the North Sea, before being sent to Madeira on salvage station. *Seaman*, *Lady Vera* and *Lady Theresa* were at Loch Kishorn until March when the latter two were relieved by *Tradesman*. *Statesman* was with Shell and *Englishman* along with the Star Offshore Tugs were all kept busy with the Dutch contractor Heerema. A company re-organisation resulted in United Towing becoming part of the North British Maritime Group which also purchased the Cochrane shipyard at Selby where so many of the towing fleet had been built. This important acquisition was marked with the placing of an order for two new ocean tugs to be delivered the following year as the *Irishman* and *Yorkshireman*.

The contribution made by United Towing during the Icelandic fishing dispute resulted in the award of an MBE to Charles Noble, one of the tug masters who gave such distinguished service protecting the trawler fleet. Acknowledgement of the commercial enterprise of United Towing (Ocean Tugs) Ltd. came with the Queen's Award for Export as a tribute to a high level of dollar earnings. Lord Halifax made the official presentation on 10 June to Sir Basil A. Parkes, President of the North British Maritime Group at a ceremony in King William House, the headquarters of United Towing between 1976 and 1985.

During the previous year Star Offshore Services had placed an order for a flat-topped materials barge with Dredge and Marine Shipyard, Penryn, Cornwall. The same company had already built *Moorsman*, but their yard being restricted in size could only cope with their new commission by constructing it in two sections to make up a barge measuring 300 feet by 90 feet, the standard size employed in the offshore industry. By the Spring of 1977 they were nearly completed, but the yard had gone into liquidation, and Falmouth Docks and Engineering were given the task of finishing off and then joining the two sections. The barge had a large engine room to house ballast pumps as well as the anchor machinery and a gross tonnage of 4,792. She was named *Bargeman*, the tug of that name having been re-christened *Riverman*. Delivered on 13 May she was immediately chartered to a Dutch offshore company who retained her services until November, when *Winchman* towed her back to Falmouth for laying up. At the end of August the Tetney monobuoy which had been towed to Rotterdam for docking had been brought back to the Humber by *Seaman*, which later picked up a barge for Wimpey Marine, loaded with construction equipment. Sailing from Tilbury on 26 September they arrived in Trinidad on 1 November, after which *Seaman* proceeded to Conakry to pick up a tow for delivery to Las Palmas in December. Early in September *Statesman* on her way through the Mediterranean to the Suez Canal was sent to assist the Iranian vessel *Ayra Seem* aground on a reef in the Strait of Jabal at the southern end of the Gulf of Suez. A Smit Lloyd supply vessel was also chartered, and under the direction of a salvage superintendent sent from Hull some of the cargo was off-loaded and the vessel eventually refloated on 12 September. *Statesman* then towed the *Katina Mattheou*

Superman.

from the south Egyptian port of Safaja to Suez before going to Jeddah to help the Salvage Association in handling a stern-loading ro-ro vessel. The *Seaspeed Dora* had taken a severe list with a large influx of water and the local port authority lacked the facilities to deal with her. After considerable bureaucratic problems over documentation she was towed away for repairs, arriving at Suez on 1 November. It was 18 November before *Seaspeed Dora* cleared the canal and four days later she arrived at Piraeus for docking. The *Statesman* together with *Welshman* delivered a tow to Barcelona in heavy weather, before returning to Piraeus to collect *Seaspeed Dora* on 20 December for final delivery at Gothenburg on 11 January 1978.

Lloydsman steaming southwards in the North Atlantic was ordered early in October to Bonny River, Nigeria to assist the bulk carrier *Areti*, and a team from the salvage department in Hull went out to organise the recovery attempt. The vessel was grounded well out of the main shipping channel which made the approach for the tugs difficult, but on 10 October *Areti* was successfully refloated. In the middle of November *Lloydsman* and the salvage team refloated a fishing vessel, *Tah Yuan No.1* aground near Abidjan. The same month Land and Marine completed their contract in Uruguay and *Superman* towed the materials barge *Odinn* to Santos to engage in laying a sewage outfall pipe. Meanwhile *Englishman* was towing a work platform from Le Havre to Penrhyn, Menai Strait, but the platform developed structural problems and was taken into Falmouth. It was not until 11 February the following year that it finally arrived off Bangor towed there by *Lady Moira*. The Star Offshore tugs were kept busy, but unfortunately the main charterer had decided to invest in building his own tugs which would soon be available to take over the offshore contracts. At the end of December after changing crew and reprovisioning at Las Palmas, *Seaman* proceeded to Dakar where after refuelling she picked up a tow. After a stop-over at Las Palmas, *Seaman* delivered the vessel to Haugesund, Norway, in March the following year.

On December 16 the sister ships *Venoil* and *Venpet*, two super-tankers each more than 150,000 tons gross, collided in fog twenty-five miles off the South African coast. After temporary repairs the *Lloydsman* towed *Venpet* the 8,100 miles from Cape Town to Nagasaki where she had originally been built; they departed on 5 February 1978 and arrived in Japan on 17 May. *Statesman* collected a large cement construction craft from Bremerhaven in January which was taken to Nigeria arriving at Lagos on 28 February. *Englishman* was also sent to Nigeria for offshore work before towing a tender from Warri to Curacao in the Caribbean. *Statesman* sailed on southwards calling in at Walvis Bay before proceeding to Singapore, where she arrived early in May. She then towed a barge to Port Said where her load of dredging material was discharged, and *Statesman* continued with the empty barge for delivery at Ijmuiden. On arrival in Hull at the end of July the tug was sold to Selco Salvage of Singapore. At the beginning of 1978 *Serviceman* towed a tanker from Antwerp to Vinaroz, Spain, and then collected another vessel at Limassol, Cyprus, which was delivered at Hamburg on 6 March. The Star Offshore tugs were all off charter during the quiet winter months, but *Welshman* was kept busy with local tows in the Mediterranean, in between which she was keeping salvage station. She then took a loaded material barge from Amsterdam to Aquaba and returned with the empty barge which was handed over to *Scotsman* off Malta. The latter arrived with her charge at Flushing on 26 March. During March *Winchman* was sent out from Falmouth to assist a German tug with a semi-submersible rig being towed in the face of continuing bad weather. Unfortunately *Winchman* suffered mechanical problems with her towing gear, and *Guardsman* took her place remaining with the rig until it was well clear of coastal waters. At the end of the month *Lady Alma* and *Lady Sarah* were chartered by the Department of Trade and Industry for anti-pollution duties. A tanker had run aground and spilt her load on the French coast, threatening the whole of the English

Seaman *in dry dock.*

Channel. The tugs were based at St. Peter Port, Guernsey, but the menace retreated and they were released after only a week. On 30 March Cochranes delivered *Irishman*, 641 tons gross, with two Ruston engines developing 4380 b.h.p., twin screws and a bow thruster. Her towing winch was a new concept, the Lebus system, with the lead-out of the towing wire always remaining in the same position; the wire was on two inclined drums and then ran onto the storage drums. Her maximum bollard pull was 70 tonnes.

Serviceman left Cherbourg in mid-April towing a submersible transportation barge with the rig Orion as deck cargo bound for Sao Louis on the north east coast of Brazil where they arrived on 26 May. Earlier that same year Orion had grounded in the Channel Isles after breaking her tow, but she was successfully salvaged and transferred to another barge for her journey to South America. *Englishman*, after completing her tow from Nigeria to Curacao, changed her crew at Kingston, Jamaica, before departing with a transportation barge for delivery to Japan. After negotiating the Panama Canal she sailed on to Honolulu where she was relieved of her tow. She then took charge of another transportation barge from a Japanese tug and headed back to Panama. Again continuing shuttle fashion, *Englishman* returned towards Honolulu relieving another tug of her tow before finally proceeding back to Panama. *Serviceman* took over and *Englishman* put into Acapulco for repairs, then doing a couple of tows in the Caribbean area out of Trinidad.

A collision in early May off the Norfolk coast resulted in the *Eleni V*, a fully loaded tanker of 12680 tons, breaking in two. The stern section was taken in tow by a Dutch tug and brought up in the river Maas, but the bow section, abandoned by her owners, remained both a source of pollution and a navigational hazard in the shipping lanes. Chartered by the Department of Trade and Industry, *Scotsman* connected with the hulk on 7 May and managed to keep it under control and away from the coast until it could be decided what to do with it.

On 17 May *Guardsman* was also chartered and towed the shattered hull into the middle of the North Sea where it capsized and sank on 30 May.

Superman, still in charge of the pipe pulling barge *Odinn*, moved down towards the Magellan Straits where she commenced work on an oil pipe at Rio Gallegos. The job was completed at the end of September and after calling at Montevideo for repairs *Superman* proceeded to Puerto Cabello, where she was sold on 1 December to Venecia Ship Services of Venezuela. *Seaman*, after a period laid up in Hull, had been sold to the same company on 22 August. On 3 July Cochranes delivered *Yorkshireman*, sister ship to the *Irishman*, bringing a well-loved name back into the fleet. *Welshman* came out of the Mediterranean with a tow from Marseilles to Douala in the Cameroon, and then returned with a vessel from Lagos to Barcelona, stopping at Las Palmas on the way. After completion of this tow *Welshman* sailed to Ostend where on 6 October she was sold to Knights tugs of Rochester.

Late on the afternoon of 12 October the Greek tanker *Christos Bitas* (formerly *Panachaikon*), heading through the St. Georges Channel, struck the Hats and Barrels rocks east of the Smalls lighthouse. *Guardsman*, on station at Falmouth, was soon in the vicinity and on arrival offered help to the damaged vessel, which however refloated without assistance and resumed her course for Belfast. A short time later it became apparent that the vessel was settling in the water and she threatened to become a major pollution hazard by the loss of her cargo of 35,000 tons of Iranian Crude Oil. On Friday 13 October the tanker had a fourteen degree list and her bow was under water, when after agreeing terms under Lloyds standard forms *Guardsman* hitched a line to her. The *Christos Bitas* was then towed away from the main shipping lanes, whilst a response was awaited from the British and Irish governments both of which had been officially requested by United Towing to provide a safe port of refuge for the stricken vessel. The Irish authorities reported that they had no port capable of handling this casualty and the British Government asked for more time to consider all the possible implications. *Christos Bitas* was a Greek owned tanker, insured in America, on charter to a British company (partly owned by the Government) and handled by agents in London and New York, *en route* from Holland to Belfast. This confusion of international interests caused the Department of Trade to intervene under section 12 of the Prevention of Pollution Act of 1971, in order to resolve the situation as soon as possible and prevent an environmental disaster. The tanker *Esso York* was moored alongside and shortly before midnight on 14 October pumped out the bulk of the crude oil from the *Christos Bitas*. Next morning the tug *Lady Theresa* arrived with further salvage crew and equipment and the BP tanker *British Dragoon* was manoeuvred into position to take aboard what remained of the cargo, whilst *Guardsman* held the tow line of the crippled tanker in a westerly gale reaching force nine. *British Dragoon* left the scene on the 22nd and a major pollution risk had been averted. After considerable discussion, the Department of Trade decided that the *Christos Bitas* should be towed to deep water in the Atlantic and sunk. So on 26 October the *Guardsman* proceeded into the open sea with an escort of British and Irish naval ships. Five days later with the tanker listing heavily to starboard, storm force winds imminent and *Guardsman's* towing speed down to only two knots, it was obvious that they could not reach the location that had been decided on. At 15.40 hours on 31 October Capt. A. J. Oakley, salvage master, reported that *Christos Bitas* had gone down in 2,600 fathoms of water some three hundred miles off Fastnet.

By early November *Lloydsman* had completed towing the rig *Ron Tapmeyer* from Singapore to Palawan. Returning to home waters, she was called to the *Global Mariner*, a 12,000 ton vessel aground north of Massawa. She arrived in what was at the time a war zone and with an escort of gun boats and helicopters. The casualty was refloated and *Lloydsman* continued on her passage home in the new year. *Yorkshireman*, after her delivery in July, spent some time on salvage station and engaged in coastal tows, but after a rig move proceeded in December from Rotterdam with a dredging craft which was brought up in Guadeloupe at the end of January 1979.

CHAPTER NINE

THE FALKLANDS CAMPAIGN AND
A MONSTER TOW

As 1980 began *Irishman* was in the Persian Gulf awaiting orders off Bahrain and *Yorkshireman* arrived at Antwerp on 6 January with the Liberian registered *Serene Med*, a vessel which had been aground off the north African coast. *Guardsman* did two coastal tows, a Wimpey materials barge and a gravel dredger. Then with *Serviceman* she went to Bilbao for inspection prior to being sold on 29 January to the Alianza Naviera of Argentina. *Scotsman* commenced various north sea barge tows early in January and *Bargeman* was chartered by Brown and Root also for operation in home waters. *Englishman*, after repairs in Gibraltar, proceeded early in February to attempt a salvage job off the Moroccan coast near Casablanca. Here she came under fire from an aircraft and was buzzed by helicopters, so the operation was abandoned and *Englishman* sailed to Las Palmas. New orders directed her through the Panama Canal to Manzanillo where she arrived on 13 March, departing two days later with a tow for Piraeus. *Irishman* left the Gulf for Suez and towed a vessel to Port Sudan. She then called at Jeddah for fuel before taking the *Lord Byron* from Berbera, Somalia, to Piraeus through the Suez Canal. *Englishman* returned to Ismailia to pick up a barge for delivery to Malta.

During 1978 United Towing had invited tenders for a new super tug with facilities for anchor handling and the ability to take on board rig anchors and crown buoys. The order was given to the Chung Wah shipyard in Hong Kong, who completed the new vessel named *Salvageman* in 1980. This vessel, enormous for a tug, is 210 feet long with a 46 foot beam and weighs in at 1598 tons gross. Her four, twelve cylinder Ruston engines develop 11,280 b.h.p.

with two variable pitch propellers in nozzles which give a bollard pull of 170 tons.

Soon after delivery on 19th April she was contracted to tow a dredger from Hiroshima to Port Said. *Salvageman* left Japan on 3 May just as the south-west monsoon was beginning to pick up strength across the Indian Ocean. After refuelling at Singapore the somewhat waterlogged dredger was taken into the lee of an atoll in the Maldives for pumping out, before finally arriving in the Suez Canal on 4 July. Leaving her tow in Egypt, *Salvageman* arrived in her home port for the first time on 18 July and after some refitting went to Stavanger the following month to do her bollard pull before arriving in Aberdeen to offer her services to the offshore industry.

Yorkshireman, keeping a salvage watch in the Mediterranean, towed a disabled tanker into Cadiz and then went on stand-by at Almeria under contract to a construction company. She picked up a barge for towing to the North Sea. *Scotsman*, after towing HMS *Guernsey* into Lerwick, followed by another tow to Gijon, joined *Yorkshireman* in convoy off northern Spain. *Bargeman* completed her charter to Brown and Root and sailed to Rotterdam on a new contract with Shell Exploration. In mid-August *Yorkshireman* commenced the tow of a loaded cement construction barge from Falmouth to the Persian Gulf. The start of the Iraqi-Iranian war caused her to anchor off the Omani coast to await further instructions, and the barge was eventually delivered to Aquaba in the Red Sea on 31 December. *Englishman* arrived in Piraeus after her journey from Manzanillo and then picked up a cargo barge from Odessa in the Black Sea, which she hauled to Rotterdam.

After a number of rig shifts *Englishman* commenced a tow fom Holland to Catania, Sicily. From there she sailed to Malta for a rig move, and then towed barges from Port Said to Sicily before embarking on a long run across the Atlantic to New Orleans. At the end of October *Englishman* left New Orleans with another tow and headed back for Piraeus, where she arrived on 15 December. After this period of hectic activity she proceeded to Naples and was sold to local owners on 22 December 1980. Early in December *Scotsman* left Bordeaux for West Africa and after her charge was unloaded at Gabon, returned back to France. *Lady Debbie* and *Lady Moira* were regularly in demand and frequently helped the ocean tugs with rig moves.

Yorkshireman began the new year by picking up a disabled vessel in the gulf of Suez which she delivered to Malta. In February she joined *Salvageman* and *Irishman* to connect with a large concrete structure afloat in a Norwegian fjord. *Irishman* then commenced towing Land and Marine's *Balder* from Leith to Panama, where she srrived in April. From there she sailed to Puerto Limon to collect a tow bound for Brownsville, Texas, then took a small rig from the Caribbean to Ireland, arriving at Money Point on 9 July. *Scotsman* picked up a vessel off Cape St. Vincent and towed her to Split, Yugoslavia, before sailing on to Abidjan, Ivory Coast in April. From here *Scotsman* took an offshore vessel to Malta and after further work in the Mediterranean docked at Piraeus on 14 July, where she was sold to local owners.

Salvageman took charge of the tanker *Texaco Great Britain* (125,942 tons) at Dakar and arrived with her nearly three months later on 26 June at Singapore. The Company's Ocean tug fleet, consisting of three vessels, *Salvageman*, *Yorkshireman* and *Irishman*, was kept busy up till the end of the year. *Salvageman* arrived back at Hull on 25 July and went with *Irishman* to Norway to pick up a concrete structure known as *Statfjord B*, before engaging a rig. *Irishman* headed for Tunisia to tow *Bargeman* to Sharjah in the United Arab Emirates where they arrived on 21 October. A week later *Bargeman* was towed back to the Mediterranean to a location off the Libyan coast before berthing her at Ravenna.

Salvageman was contracted at the start of 1982 to haul the McDermott derrick barge DB100 to the Leman bank for piling operations. Early in February the barge was towed into the Moray Firth and *Yorkshireman* took another McDermott barge from here to Cadiz, which she

then brought back with pre-fabricated modules for assembly at Ardersier. *Irishman* left Ravenna and after a stop-over in Algeciras arrived in the Tyne on 21 January, where the *Bargeman* was put into dry dock. The latter was soon in demand and commenced a short charter from Hartlepool. *Lady Moira* and *Lady Debbie* were employed throughout in a variety of coastal tows and rig-shifting. *Irishman* was put on salvage station in the English Channel, and in mid-March sailed to Lisbon to pick up a tow, which she delivered in Rotterdam on 24 March, before starting a charter with Heerema, the Dutch offshore contractors.

The start of 1982 may have been a routine one for the United Towing fleet, but dramatic events following the Argentine invasion of the Falklands resulted in the deployment of the three biggest salvage tugs to the South Atlantic. On 6 April at 12.15 pm, the Company's flagship *Salvageman* was requisitioned by the Department of Trade to sail with the task force then being assembled for the recapture of the Falklands.

She was at that time undergoing repairs at Aberdeen prior to continuing with her long term contract to handle the barge DB100 for McDermotts. Instead *Salvageman* proceeded with maximum speed to Portsmouth where between Friday 9th and Tuesday 13th April she was bunkered, provisioned and given a fresh crew. On 7 April *Yorkshireman*, whilst towing the barge P10 from Ardersier to the Magnus site, was also called up for a active service and directed to Lerwick. At the same time *Irishman*, then in the Dutch port of Flushing to undertake a barge tow to Finland, also received instructions to join the task force. No modications were made to the three tugs as they were eventually going to carry out the same sort of tasks as in their normal peace-time roles, but they were equipped with a plentiful supply of salvage gear, along with submersible pumps, generators, air compressors and some special Naval Salvage gear. *Salvageman* and *Irishman* left Portsmouth on Easter Sunday 10th April and *Yorkshireman* departed three days later, all heading for Ascension Island,

Guardsman involved in barge tow.

Euroman towing the tanker **Gallant Colocotronis**.

Christos Bitos, down by the head.

Seaman, *free running.*

Lady Debbie *(foreground) and* **Lady Moira**.

99

on the first leg of the journey south. Progress was uneventful, except that *Yorkshireman* needed new radio equipment which was air-dropped by an RAF *Hercules* transport plane. *Salvageman* arrived at Ascension Island, refuelled and proceeded to Tristan de Cunha, some two thousand miles further south, but her two companions made a stop-over of six days before sailing together for the same destination where they arrived on 10 May.

In the meantime, South Georgia had been recaptured and *Salvageman* and the naval tug *Typhoon* were ordered there to assist HMS *Sheffield* one of the first casualties of the war. Nothing was found of the vessel which had in fact been sunk and was a total loss. After refuelling *Salvageman* skirted some two hundred miles east of the Falklands working with the repair ship *Stena Seaspread*, handling various battle-damaged ships. On 12 May HMS *Glasgow* had been hit by a 1000 lb. bomb which passed right through her engine room, but thankfully failed to explode. *Salvageman* was ordered to stand by but was then called to help the *Atlantic Conveyor* with all possible speed after she had been struck by an Exocet missile. On arrival there was little that could be done and *Salvageman* rejoined *Yorkshireman* and *Irishman* on 24 May in a holding 'pen' 40 miles square, to the east of the Falklands. Here the tugs would be safe from the enemy attacks and could hold themselves in readiness for further duties.

It was decided to assess the salvage possibilities of *Atlantic Conveyor*, but *Irishman* reached her only after struggling for nearly fifteen hours through fog, low visibility and a 10 to 12 feet swell. The crew managed to get a line aboard but the tow soon parted. A second line was connected at about 1 am on 28 May, but the gear parted for the second time and *Atlantic Conveyor* sank. Subsequently Able Seaman D. P. Betts and Able Seaman G. Bales, two of *Irishman's* crew, were awarded the British Empire Medal for their bravery in twice boarding the ravaged vessel to secure a line. On 5 June *Salvageman* and *Yorkshireman* headed back to South Georgia to begin work on the Argentinian submarine *Santa Fe*, which had been beached and scuttled in Grytviken harbour after being struck on 25 April by an AS12 wire-guided missile. *Salvageman* then joined the frigate *Yarmouth*, and the tanker RFA *Olmeda* to repossess South Thule which had been occupied illegally by a small contingent of Argentinians since 1976. No resistance was offered by the small force of naval officers and ratings who were on the island and Captain Alan Stockwell, Master of the *Salvageman*, was present as an official witness to the surrender. *Irishman* was with HMS *Ambuscade* recovering troops and equipment while *Salvageman* and *Yorkshireman* returned to the *Santa Fe* which was lying partially sunk alongside the jetty at Grytviken. The salvage crew worked below decks amidst a foul mixture of battery acid, rotting food, sewage and diesel oil. In addition the hull had a twenty degree list and there were quantities of potentially unstable explosives lying around. The whole operation took two weeks with the pumps working night and day in temperatures well below freezing, but the submarine was successfully removed to a safe beaching site. *Irishman* was occupied in Fox Bay, West Falkland, salvaging the 3828 tons *Bahia Buen Suceso* which had grounded after an attack in the middle of May. She was refloated at the first attempt and towed to San Carlos bay after which the *Irishman* sailed to Port Pleasant off Fitzroy to bring the landing ship *Sir Tristram* off the beach and re-anchor her. *Irishman* then rejoined *Salvageman* and *Yorkshireman* and they continued to work under navy instructions docking the numerous merchant ships bringing in supplies and co-operating with teams of divers involved in clearance work. All three tugs remained in the South Atlantic long after most of the other requisitioned vessels had returned home. *Irishman* was the first of the trio to be released by the Ministry of Defence and she arrived back in Hull on 2 December to receive the full publicity treatment from the press, television, and radio. Three days later she sailed for the Tyne to undergo a much needed refit after her exertions in the fearsome climate of the South Atlantic. During her dry-docking *Irishman* was fitted out with

Salvageman with *Santa Fé* alongside.

Euroman leaving Hull.

Atlantic Conveyor.

The 'Big One'! tow out of Andoc Production platform.
From left to right, **Guardsman, Linesman (Tempest** *and* **Typhoon** *of Bureau Wijsmuller)* **Winchman** *and* **Serviceman***.*

satellite communications equipment, a HIAB hydraulic crane of six ton capacity and a new inflatable workboat. Also while on the Tyne she received a brass plaque from the Royal Navy in recognition of the outstanding bravery and seamanship of the crew in the Falklands campaign. After refitting and completion of trials, *Irishman* was in fact immediately requisitioned by the Department of Trade and sailed southwards once again.

The loss of the ocean fleet on Government service persuaded United Towing to hire the *Normand Rock* a 6600 b.h.p. twin screw tug which was renamed *Euroman*. The controllable pitch propellers in Kort nozzles were driven by two Winchman engines and she was capable of handling anchors over the open stern. After lengthy repairs at Ramsgate the *Euroman*, with a bollard pull of 92 tons, was available for charter in the commercial market. It was the end of 1983 before *Yorkshireman* returned to Hull after fifteen months of continuous service in and around the Falklands. Peter Rimmer, the Master, was presented with a brass plaque by Murray Walker, director of marine services to the Royal Navy, to express the Admiralty's thanks for her reliable and efficient service under the most extreme conditions. After refitting on the Tyne she resumed her commercial duties alongside *Euroman*.

On completion of refitting, *Yorkshireman* was to be involved in commercial activities again on a truly heroic scale. Norwegian contractors had designed a rig for Mobil, a huge mass of concrete, named *Statfjord C* Gravity Base Structure, with a maximum length of 148.2 metres, and four shafts, to support a deck structure, extending to a height of 110 metres. *Statfjord C* had an estimated displacement of 615,000 tons and a draught of 63 feet and such a tow being beyond the resources of even United Towing, or any of its principal rivals on the continent, acting independently, *Yorkshireman* and *Euroman* were hired as part of an international consortium. United's Norman Storey was the senior tow master who was aboard the rig in radio communications with the nine tugs which had a combined bollard pull of

900 tonnes. On Wednesday 18 January the tow began in perfect weather conditions and proceeded slowly along a twisting route around the islands of Boknfjorden and Nedstrandfjord, from Stavanger to Vats. The maximum speed was 2.5 knots but most of the time they moved at no more than .5 knots and it took 49 hours to cover the 46 miles after six months of meticulous planning. The deck-mating of the whole structure took place in February and in June Captain Storey was again in command for the *biggest tow ever made* taking the complete structure 250 miles to a location north west of Bergen. Eight tugs were engaged to bring *Statfjord C* into position at 6.27 on Whit Sunday morning to complete a job requiring all the skill and expertise of the most experienced tug men. It was an achievement every bit as remarkable as anything that had occurred in the Falklands, though scarcely noticed by the world's press.

Not until Friday 22 June 1984, two years and four months after her departure, did *Salvageman* once again enter the Humber, escorted by *Lady Stephanie* and *Lady Susan*, which saluted her with massive jets of water from their fire-fighting equipment, which reached high in the air over *Salvageman's* superstructure. After her 7500 miles journey she looked in surprisingly good condition and entered the lock gate of King George dock to the cheers of an anxious and excited crowd. Her Captain was Ian Stockwell who was also in command when she had rst joined the task force in April 1982. It was decided at *Salvageman* would be refitted in a local yard. Leaving her berth at No.6 shed she was towed by *Lady Marina* of Humber Tugs to the river Hull where she was soon to fill the Central Dry Dock of Ruscador Ltd. An Ulstein shark jaw was fitted to allow her to take on board the largest rig anchors and she was also provided with satellite communications equipment. *Salvageman* completed her river trials with few problems and painted with the new North British company logo, she sailed for the Thames. Here, tied up alongside HMS *Belfast*, opposite Tower pier, she received specially invited guests from government and industry. The Right Hon. John

Statesman towing rig off South Africa.

Galveston Key under tow by **Yorkshireman**, **Seaman** and a Dutch tug.

The former United Towing headquarters, Nelson Street.

Salvageman *towing jack-up rig.*

Gary Bales and Dennis Betts.

Euroman.

Statfjord C and route of tow.

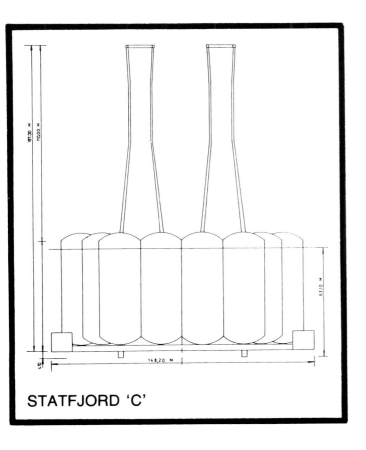

STATFJORD 'C'

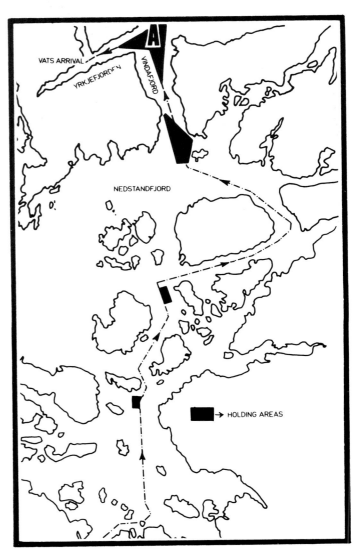

Stanley MP., Minister of State for the Armed Forces, presented the tug and her crew with battle honours before *Salvageman* departed for Portsmouth. After taking on stores and fuel she directed her path to the South Atlantic again to finish the job on the Argentinian submarine *Santa Fe*, which was to be refloated and sunk in deep water to remove the hazard of munitions in a state of corrosion.

On Christmas Eve 1984, the *Implacable* of Alexandra Towing on passage to the Falklands sank in heavy seas with the tragic loss of her chief enginer. *Euroman*, at the time working in the North Sea, was chartered as an urgent replacement and after re-provisioning at Rotterdam she too headed south on 31 December. Captain Rimmer took command but the crew who were nearing the end of their tour of duty were not replaced till she reached Ascension Island in mid-January. The twenty-seven day journey, fortunately without mishap,. was achieved at an average speed of 12.4 knots.

CHAPTER TEN

A DOWNTURN, BUT A NEW ERA DAWNING

Experience and high quality seamanship have always been hallmarks of the United Towing and Humber Tugs tradition and this was never more in evidence when just before Christmas 1985 near tragedy struck the *Lady Vera*. She and *Lady Moira* were towing the 30,000 ton cargo vessel *Adelina* from Immingham to Flushing when her tow sheave parted causing the wire to jam and the tug to heel over and take in water. *Lady Vera* then collided with her tow which fortunately parted the wire allowing her to level up again. Meanwhile *Lady Moira* under the command of Capt. Cyril Reibbitt managed to keep control of the tow. The *Lady Stephanie* had been sent to give assistance, but before she arrived *Lady Vera* managed to regain some power and start making her way back to Immingham with a very shaken crew. Thankfully there were no casualties, but if the tugs had been further into the tow the situation could well have had fatal results. The *Adelina* was finally delivered to Flushing by the *Lady Moira* and the *Lady Debbie*, with additional support from the ocean going salvage tug *Euroman*.

Early that year the *Seaman*, a new multi-purpose tug, entered the Humber Tugs fleet, having been launched by Lady Fieldhouse, wife of the First Sea Lord. She was able to combine many roles never before available in a tug of her size, including anchor-handling, rig-moving and docking work. It was appropriately named since sixty years earlier her namesake had made company history by being the first United Towing vessel to work in the South Atlantic when she left Boston, Lincs. on 16 May 1925, bound for Buenos Aires with two former minesweepers under tow.

In the early summer of 1985 most of the Humber Tugs vessels were busily employed in a wide range of duties, though offshore business was very slack around this time. A glut on the world oil market had brought about a cutback in production and exploration in the North Sea. After extensive repairs at Goole the sea-going *Lady Vera* returned to service and was based in Hull replacing *Masterman*, which had been placed on bareboat charter with the Holyhead Towing Co. for offshore work on the west coast of Scotland. *Irishman* and *Euroman* were still under MOD contract in the South Atlantic, while the flag ship of the United Towing fleet, *Salvageman*, was towing the five-legged, pentagon-type, semi-submersible rig *Asterie* from Sicily to the Campos field off Brazil. *Seaman* by this time had completed her first charter with Shell Exploration in the Fulmar gas field, where she proved her worth against much larger tugs. Also at this time the Company headquarters moved out of King William House in the Market Place and relocated in Boston House, at the entrance to St. Andrew's Dock, previously the head office of Boston Deep Sea Fisheries belonging to the Parkes family. This had a certain appropriateness since Basil Parkes had taken a controlling interest in United Towing in 1962 and was responsible for rebuilding the Company and equipping it with a modern fleet able to compete with their continental rivals.

Meanwhile *Yorkshireman* had sailed from Dover to take up salvage station off Deal and then departed for the Hook of Holland where she had been contracted to tow the first of two halves of a dry dock for Nedbarges from Rotterdam to Norfolk, Virginia. The contract lasted from 16 July to 30 August, and when she arrived back in United Kingdom waters she lay on salvage station off the Humber for some three days before finally being orderd into Hull on 2 September. While all this was happening *Irishman* and *Salvageman*, recently joined by *Euroman*, were working in the South Atlantic on charter to the MOD. *Irishman* had remained on long-term contract, while *Salvageman* had returned to complete work on the Argentine submarine *Santa Fé* which she had beached during the early part of the Falklands conflict. Under the command of Captain John Bold, *Salvageman* working alongside the naval auxiliary vessel *Goosander*, refloated the submarine from a position just outside Grytviken harbour where she had subsequently sunk. The *Santa Fé* was then towed out into deep water and sunk again in an area where she would no longer be a hazard to shipping; the task was completed on 20 February 1986.

Yorkshireman on station in the Gulf of Suez completed the salvage of the British bulk carrier *Benhope* under Lloyds open form. Despite severe hull damage she was escorted into Aqaba where a Marine Services team led by Captain Dennis Pearce successfully off-loaded her cargo of soya meal and corn. Temporary repairs enabled the *Benhope* to proceed to Piraeus for permanent repairs.

The river tugs were still very busy, as were the sea-going vessels, particularly in the southern sector of the North Sea. In the early hours of 12 January the *Lady Elizabeth*, on her way to carry out a rig-move, picked up distress calls from the West German coaster *Pamir II*. The crew had already taken to the life rafts by the time the tug had arrived on the scene and were eventually picked up by the Flamborough lifeboat. Despite heavy seas and driving snow the crew of the *Lady Elizabeth* managed to secure a line and brought the stricken vessel safely into Hull. Not long afterwards her sister tug, the *Lady Constance*, went to the assistance of the 499 ton coaster *Betty C* near the Inner Dowsing light vessel where she lay with disabled engines. She too was successfully towed into Hull and *Lady Moira* followed this by bringing in the 1495 ton *Inger* with a cargo of Scottish potatoes, after suffering engine failure near the Rough gas field.

Following operations at Methil, United Towing's mooring barge *Moorsman* went aground in gale force winds while under tow by the tug *Masterman*. The tow parted some eleven miles off the Northumberland coast and *Moorsman* driffted until she ran aground one and a half miles north-east of Alnmouth, close to Seaton Point. Captain Dennis Pearce was sent from Hull with a Marine Services team to co-ordinate the refloating attempts as soon as conditions eased, but operations were made very difficult by an onshore easterly gale. The sea-going tug *Lady Debbie*, which had just completed a tow to Teesport, was diverted to give assistance and at high water on 13 February, some four days after running ashore, *Moorsman* was brought off and towed back to the Humber for dry-docking at Goole.

All the ocean-going tugs were being kept busy and holding their own in the highly competitive North Sea domain. *Salvageman* was involved towing the rig *Asterie* from early May until the end of July 1985, and after completion remained in and around West Indies until 26 November, when she sailed for Turk Island to give assistance to a grounded merchantman. The vessel was the 10,000 ton *Marianthe* (ex *City of Liverpool*) and had been travelling at about 17 knots when she struck a reef in the Turks and Caicos group, sustaining damage to her bottom plates. She was travelling without cargo, so that there was no way in which she could be lightened preparatory to any attempt at pulling her off. Many salvage experts thought it would be impossible to save the *Marianthe*, but United Towing yet again despatched Captain Dennis Pearce, senior salvage superintendent, to advise on the steps to be taken. On 2 December, following a favourable survey, Mike Lacey, United Towing's Managing Director, signed a Lloyds Open Form for the refloating of the vessel.

The *Marianthe* was actually trapped within a series of reefs and the salvage team had first to establish a safe channel, which was marked with a series of eight buoys. Even then there was at times only two feet clearance beneath the keel of the *Salvageman* and it was impossible to make a direct approach to the casualty. Over half a mile of 64mm tow wire had to be paid out, supported by buoyancy bags, and Captain pearce used the 550 tonnes of fuel on board to achieve the best trim. During the space of three tides *Salvageman*, exerting a pull of 168 tonnes, succeeded in moving the vessel slowly astern into the marked channel and she was finally refloated on Thursday 5 December. Redelivery to her owners was to prove somewhat difficult since they were unwilling to

Irishman free running in the Humber.

Winchman working with a crane barge.

accept the vessel in its immediate location. The *Marianthe* was therefore towed 850 miles to Jacksonville on the Atlantic coast of Florida, where she was handed over to local harbour tugs on Tusday 10 December. *Salvageman* was then ordered to sail to Port Arthur in order to make a crew change, and then headed for Sabine Pass for her next tow, a rig named the *Aleutian Key*, destined for Santos, Brazil.

Ocean-going salvage tugs are very expensive to run. The *Salvageman* might cost up to a million pounds a year to cover fuel, maintenance and wages. The Company is constantly seeking new jobs so that there is as little dead time between each contract as possible. *Irishman* and *Euroman* remained in the South Atlantic while *Yorkshireman* was on salvage station off Gibraltar. North Sea oil and gas operations kept the sea-going tugs busy, and as 1985 drew to a close business looked in good shape for the new year ahead.

In the early months of 1986 the sea-going and ocean-going side of operations continued to do well and an upturn in business in Hull and Immingham also kept the fleet of harbour tugs busy. *Yorkshireman* had remained on salvage station off Northern Spain until she was contracted under Lloyds Open Form to refloat the Greek-registered bulk carrier *Jimmy*, which was aground near Le Havre in France. This 25,231 tonne deadweight vessel was one of a number of victims of the severe weather which had lashed Europe, causing many casualties. The efforts of a salvage team from United Towing and the sea-going tug *Seaman* enabled the vessel to be slowly shifted over successive high tides. In the early hours of 30 January, a combined pull from *Yorkshireman* and *Seaman* saw *Jimmy* completely refloated after which she was taken into Le Havre for dry-docking. *Seaman* then made for Immingham and *Yorkshireman* sailed for Dover to remain there on salvage station.

In early February *Seaman* and *Yorkshireman* teamed up again to tow the *Galveston Key* to Block 48 of the North Sea oil and gas field. *Salvageman* meanwhile was still occupied towing the *Aleutian Key* to Brazil, but after

her return home she was to have lengthy spells in dry-dock in Glasgow until completion of repairs and maintenance on 29 April. *Euroman* completed her Ministry of Defence charter and sailed for the United Kingdom on 15 June after a seventeen month stay in the Falklands waters. She returned towing the aviation fuel barge *Cubus*, her longest tow in four years of service with United Towing. Arriving in Southampton on Monday 11 August she delivered the barge and sailed on to Goole arriving on the fifteenth for a refit. Work was completed on the 17 September and *Euroman* headed down-river to Hull, where she was redelivered to her owners after some four years on charter to United Towing.

The Company was still obtaining a good share of the available jobs but the overall volume of business competed for by United Towing and their rivals had diminished considerably. Early in October 1986 therefore United Towing put *Yorkshireman* on a bareboat charter to Semco Salvage for work in the Gulf War zone.

Salvageman and *Irishman* were left to maintain the ocean-towing capacity. The name of United Towing still had an excellent standing and the Company was able to retain a good level of the market share despite a general downturn in business. The high reputation and a sound fleet of up-to-date vessels with experienced crews made the United Towing Company an obvious target for take-over, but work continued as normal whilst rumours circulated of possible bids. During October *Salvageman* was on passage from Port Said to Augusta where she had **been contracted to tow the M44 from Augusta to the Vega field for Micoperi.** After remaining on location for twenty-six days *Salvageman* finally connected with Micoperi 44 and completed the job on 24 November. *Yorkshireman* arrived in Dubai, where she was put under the Bahamian flag and handed over to Semco, while *Salvageman* sailed on to Cape Passero in Sicily to remain on salvage station until 22 December 1986.

The market for ocean-going salvage tugs was getting ever smaller and the reality for the big companies whether

Irishman and *Hullman* free running in the Humber.

British, Dutch or German, was much the same — too many large vessels and not enough work. Some jobs were still being found, however, and *Salvageman* completed the move of the *W. B. Tyson* for Reading and Bates, while *Irishman* was given an extension of her MOD contract. *Yorkshireman*, her sister tug, remained on bareboat charter with Semco in the Persian Gulf. Since there were only two large salvage tugs available, the Company was using the *Lady* tugs more and more for rig-moves and short sea tows. They performed very well in this capacity and upheld the reputation of United Towing within the towing industry.

Towards the end of January *Salvageman* was in Marseilles to tow the *Alba Marina* from Marseilles to the Adriatic, which would last until the end of February. This 140,000 tonne deadweight storage tanker was bound for the Rospomare Field in the Adriatic. On completion *Salvageman* sailed for Cape Passero where she remained on salvage station. *Seaman* meantime had been contracted to tow McDermott's barge *Goliath 10* from Dundee out to the Leeman field.

Trade was quiet for both the ocean-going and sea-going vessels through into May. *Salvageman* was on salvage station off Gibraltar and *Yorkshireman* was still on bareboat charter in the Persian Gulf.

At last the rumours of take-over proved to have substance and at the beginnig of May 1987 Howard Smith Ltd. one of Austalia's largest public companies, gained a 75% stake in the North British Maritime Group. The new Chief Executive was Dr. Ken Moss, with Philip and David Wilbraham as his deputies. United Towing was now at the beginning of a new chapter in its nearly seventy-year history. Restructuring and loss of personnel marked the initial phase of the new regime in an effort to keep the Company viable in a highly competitive market.

In July *Irishman* left the Falklands to return to the U.K., bringing to an end a period of over five years' involvement in the Falklands area with the Ministry of Defence (Navy). It was not until November 10 that *Irishman* reached the U.K. as whilst on passage she was diverted to Belem in Brazil to refloat a Taiwanese trawler, under the supervision of Captain Eric Johnson. Following this job *Irishman* proceeded to Port Harcourt in Nigeria to tow a disabled tanker to Las Palmas. She was then diverted to the Cape Verde Islands to take over the towage of a large offshore barge from a disabled Italian tug. Ultimately *Irishman* towed this barge to Brazil before resuming passage to Hull.

United Towing vessels were, however, still to be found across the globe and in January 1988 the *Ashland*, a Great Lakes steamer blown ashore in Bermuda whilst being towed from Canada to Taiwan, was successfully refloated by *Salvageman* which was in the course of towing a dry-dock from Rotterdam to Newport, U.S.A. *Irishman* and *Seaman* were involved in work with British Telecom in the Irish Sea, Bristol Channel, Western Approaches and the Bay of Biscay during the spring, and earlier *Seaman* had completed a 5,000 mile round trip towing the barge *Khakan* from Scotland to Marseilles and back to Stavanger in Norway.

During the course of 1988 *Irishman* and *Yorkshireman* were sold to Semco Salvage Co. of Singapore. This left the Company with *Salvageman*, but due to lack of remunerative work this tug was laid up in Hull for most of the year.

In March 1988 United Towing was awarded a contract to man, manage and market the Canadian flagged anchor-handling tug *Canmar Tugger II* (96 tonnes Bollard Pull). This represented a new venture for the Company which would enable it to maintain the skills and expertise built up over many years of operating its own ocean going tugs.

Since then the Company has also been awarded further management contracts in respect of the Liberian flagged anchor-handling tug *Guardsman* (100 tonnes Bollard Pull) and the Bahamian flagged anchor-handling tug *Jon Viking* (100 tonnes Bollard Pull).

All of these vessels have been used extensively in offshore operations around the U.K. by the Company and have resulted in the re-engagement of some crew members previously made redundant as a result of the sale of *Irishman* and *Yorkshireman* and the laying up of the *Salvageman*.

Recent years have witnessed some major changes within United Towing, all of which will have a profound effect on the operations of the Company in the future.

Towards the end of 1989 the Company's last ocean-going tug *Salvageman* was the largest and most powerful tug operated by United Towing and it is fitting that the days of tug ownership should finish with this vessel which served the Company so well. During her time as a United Towing tug, *Salvageman* sailed on every ocean and between ports as far apart as Yokohama and Newport, Rhode Island, and Trondheim and Grytviken, South Georgia.

The sale of *Salvageman* does not bring to an end the Company's association with the tug, as she will continue to be operated and manned by United Towing under a management agreement and as long as this agreement continues the tug will keep the name *Salvageman*. At the end of 1989 she was working in the BP Gyda oil field in the North Sea a with the great Micoperi 7000 barge crane.

Other managed tugs in the fleet now operated by United Towing include *Guardsman*, *Canmar Tugger II*, and *Jon Viking*. All of these tugs have one thing in common. They are ocean-going, anchor-handling tugs, capable of undertaking long-distance tows as well as providing support to the offshore exploration industries.

David Webb, an Australian marine engineer, arrived in January 1989 to take over from Ken Moss as Chief Executive, and in May announced plans to upgrade the eleven operational vessels of the Humber tugs fleet and the eventual replacement of up to five of them with bigger and more powerful units. In an inteview for the Business Mail (*Hull Daily Mail*, 13 December 1989) Mr. Webb announced that a £2.2 million loss on a turnover of £60m in 1988 had been transformed into a profit of £2.1m on a turnover of just £33m in 1989. The Company had discarded all its non-maritime interests, including Walfred Motors, the Joseph Bentley horticultural business, as well as Boston Deep Sea Fisheries and Norbrit Wharfage. Humber Tugs has placed a £14m order for five new harbour Tugs and these will be the most powerful tractor tugs yet to be introduced into this country. Each will be fitted with the latest shiphandling and fire-fighting equipment, designed to handle the largest crude oil carriers, chemical tankers and bulk carriers that use the Humber. Ironically, the order has had to go to McTay Marine of Merseyside since the Company's own yard, Cochranes of Selby, is currently too busy to take on this commitment.

At the end of 1989 there was another change in that Howard Smith Ltd. acquired the remaining shares in the North British Maritime Group Ltd. held by the Wilbraham family. United Towing is now, therefore, a wholly owned subsidiary of Howard Smith Ltd. of Sydney, Australia. It is singularly appropriate that the founder of this Australian company sailed from England in 1854 in the Hull-built schooner *Express*, as one of many who were then flocking to the rich gold-fields 'down under'.

The salvage division of Howard Smith was formerly called Austpac Salvage, but in 1989 they acquired the name of an Australian company with historical salvage links, namely United Salvage.

Apart from tug management the decade of the eighties ended with a busy period for United Towing's Salvage Division. During the Summer of 1989 Captain Mark Hoddinott and Captain Eric Johnson were both involved in a major salvage operation on the west coast of Australia. This job was conducted by Austpac Salvage and involved the stripping out of a wrecked offshore crane barge, the DB20. This unit had been stranded in an environmentally sensitive area near Dampier, and the unit had to be cleared of all materials, products, etc. which might represent a hazard to the environment.

Early on the morning of 17 September, two tankers collided some five miles off Spurn Point. The Liberian registered *Phillips Oklahoma* received a twenty-foot gash above the water line and spilled some 500 tonnes of oil.

Welshman. Englishman.

Both her and the Maltese registered *Fiona* (carrying fuel oil) caught fire and the two fire fighting tugs *Lady Susan* and *Lady Stephanie* quickly arrived on the scene. Men from the latter were winched aboard to tackle the blaze and the non-essential crew of the *Phillips Oklahoma*, which suffered a number of explosions, were taken off by the Humber lifeboat. Once the blaze was brought under control the top priority was to disperse the twenty-one mile oil slick which, thanks to the year's highest tide and a strong southerly wind, was pushed out to sea away from the Humber coastline.

The salvage operation was carried out under the supervision of Captain Dennis Pearce and ultimately the entire cargo was transferred from the stricken vessel into another tanker in the Humber anchorage.

This incident was followed by the successful salvage of an abandoned Ro-Ro vessel, *Al Kwather I*, near the Isle of Wight, carried out jointly with Klyne Tugs of Lowestoft. Just before Christmas 1989 there was another tanker salvage involving a small coastal tanker, *Eyal*, in the eastern Mediterranean. A salvage team from United Towing successfully raised this vessel which was partially sunk, towed it into port upside down, discharged her oil cargo and then righted the vessel.

As we move into the 1990s United Towing is smaller but better placed to face the future. Today the Company still has the expertise and experience gained from many years of ocean-going tug operations, together with a salvage team which has a considerable track record of success. The continued management of tugs enables the Company to maintain a core of experienced crew-members. Early 1990 also brought another change of Company headquarters. The Boston building has been vacated in favour of new premises at Marine Court, Castle Street, adjacent to the Hull Marina, which is now the headquarters of Howard Smith (U.K.)

It is difficult to forecast what the 90s might mean for a company such as United Towing. Without doubt there will always be a requirement for specialised skills in the maritime world. United Towing, under its new ownership, is now well placed to continue offering its services whether it be to move a drilling rig, salvage a disabled vessel, or provide experienced consultant personnel. One thing is certain that United Towing will now be looking to expand its operations and to move forward confidently into the 21st Century.

HOUSE FLAG AND FUNNEL COLOURS

The funnels of United Towing vessels are white with a black top, and the house flag a blue swallow-tailed pennant with a white star on which is superimposed a letter U also in blue. The five-pointed star may be indicative of the five principal components of the original United Towing fleet (see chapter 1).

T. Gray and Co. Ltd., which was the major constituent, had used a red pennant with letter G in white, and the funnels of their tugs were black with a red ring below a white ring.

The white funnel with black top seems to have been taken from the vessels of T. C. Spink, as evidenced by a photograph of the *Diplomat*, built for him in 1909 and lost in 1915. She apparently wears this livery, though in a monochrome print it is not possible to distinguish yellow (or buff) from white with absolute certainty.

Since 1982 a logo has been employed by all the companies forming the North British Maritime Group including United Towing and this is applied to the funnel, replacing a representation of the house flag used in later years. The new insignia is composed of a red compass needle pointing north over a white four-pointed star (the North Star) all within a square perimeter shape, in blue, which suggests the classic 'cupped hands' symbol. Red, white and blue are of course the national colours from the Union flag.

FLEET LIST

In 1921 there were thirty-six vessels from five constituent companies forming the fleet of the United Towing Co. Ltd. The paddle tug *Powerful* purchased December 1923 was scrapped soon after, and the *Orion* and *Winchester* acquired in 1926 were probably also scrapped without ever becoming active members of the fleet. A controlling interest in the Peter Foster Fleet was acquired in 1923, Thompson Towage was bought in 1926 and J. H. Pigott (Grimsby) in 1964. On 3 January 1970 the title of the company was altered to the simpler form United Towing Ltd. Star Offshore Services were established in 1974 as a joint venture with Blue Star line. In 1978 United Towing and various associated companies came under the umbrella of the North British Maritime Group. Control of the company has been in the hands of Howard Smith Ltd. since 1987.

The original headquarters were at 11 Nelson Street, Hull, overlooking the river near the Victoria Pier. In 1976 they were transferred to new premises at King William House, Market Place, but moved yet again in 1985 to more spacious accommodation at Boston House, St. Andrew's Dock, previously the home of Boston Deep Sea Fisheries. Early in 1990 the latter was vacated in favour of new offices in Castle Street, adjacent to the Hull Marina.

Since the continual upgrading of the fleet has expanded the capabilities of vessels allocated to Humber Tugs, many of which would have previously been designated as United Towing vessels, those vessels such as *Lady Debbie* which are registered in Hull, have been included in the list.

An anchor-handling tug joined the fleet in April 1989 and was renamed *Guardsman*, the fourth of that name. Built in 1977 as the *Hirtenturm* she was named the *Cape May* whilst working in the Gulf. She measures 710 tonnes gross, with a length of 44.7 metres and twin MAK engines, each developing 3850 b.h.p. giving 100 tonnes bollard pull. In 1985 *Seaman* (third of the name) entered service at Grimsby; built by Cochranes of Selby she has twin Ruston diesels giving her a speed of 12.5 knots. She measures 527 tonnes (gross) with a length of 33.64 metres.

The editor is pleased to acknowledge the permission of H.M. Customs & Excise to publish details from the Hull Ships registers and the help and co-operation of Mrs. S. C. Conway, Assistant to the Registrar, Portcullis House.

Please note that the dimensions indicated are in feet and inches and the *gross* tonnage of each vessel is recorded.

Grimsby vessels are not listed; only those registered in Hull.

ACE TUT (?-1962)
built : 1881
yard :
? : purchased
1961 : scrapped

ACOR (1921-1929)
built : 1896
yard : Cox and Co. Falmouth
1896-1919 : Empreza Funchalensede Cabotagem,
: Funchal
1919-1920 : His Majesty's Shipping Controller,
: London *Penguin*
1920-1921 : Premier Tow. Co. Ltd. Hull, renamed *Acor*
14.4.21 : purchased by U.T.L.
1929 : scrapped at Inverkeithing

AIRMAN (1947-1967)
built : 1945
yard : Cochrane and Sons Ltd, Selby
1945-1947 : Ministry of War Transport *Empire Clara*
1947 : purchased by U.T.L. and renamed *Airman*
1949 : re-engined
1967 : scrapped

ALEXANDRA (1926-1927)
built : 1877
yard :
1926 : purchased from Thompson Towage
1927 : scrapped

AQUILA (1921-1923)
built : 1870
yard : unknown at Bristol
1907-1921 : R. W. Wheeldon; purchased as *Pendragon*
1921 : purchased from City Steam Towing Co.
1923 : sold to Foster Tugs

AUTOCRAT (1921-1934)
built : 1915
yard : Cochrane and Sons Ltd, Selby

27.4.21 : purchased from T. C. Spink
: requisitioned for war service
19.7.34 : sank in the Humber; raised
1967 : scrapped at Belgium

BARGEMAN (1) (1962-1974)
built : 1955
yard : P. K. Harris, Appledore
1955-1962 : *Brentonian*
25.2.62 : *purchased by U.T.L. renamed Bargeman*
1974 : renamed *Riverman*
1.4.78 : transferred to Humber Tugs Ltd, Grimsby

BARGEMAN (2) (1977-1987)
built : 1977
yard : Dredge and Marine Ltd, Penryn, Cornwall
1987 : sold to Min. of Defence

BARROW (1961-   )
built : 1903
yard :
1961 : purchased from Foster Tow

BERTY (1921-1923)
built : 1914
: originally owned by R. H. Mungall
yard :
29.7.14 : sold to Premier Tug Co.
: purchased from Premier Tug Co. Ltd.
20.4.23 : sold to E. Hall & Co. Cardiff; at the same
: time resold to Portuguese owners.

BIDDY (1921-1964)
built : 1914
yard : Larne Shipbuilding Co. Larne
1921 : purchased from Premier Tug Co. Ltd.
1964 : scrapped at Queensborough

BLIGHTY (1921-1925)
built : 1880
yard : Thames Iron Works and Shipbuilding Co.
: Ltd. Blackwall

14.4.21 : purchased from Premier Tug Co. Ltd.
: (ex *Primrose*)
1925 : scrapped

BOATMAN (1927-1963)
built : 1927
yard : Cochrane and Sons Ltd. Selby
21.1.35 : sank in the Humber; raised
1963 : scrapped at Hull

BOWMAN (1952-1963)
built : 1943
yard : Richard Dunston Ltd, Thorne
1943-1948 : Min. of War Transport *TID 24*
1948-1952 : Lloyds Albert Yard and Motor Packet
: Steam Services Ltd. S'hampton *Ashford 24*
1952 : purchased
1953 : scrapped

BRAHMAN (1938-1961)
built : 1938
yard : Cochrane and Sons Ltd, Selby
26.8.39 : requisitioned by Royal Navy and renamed
: *Bat*
27.1.45 : returned in service with U.T.L.
1961 : sold to J. H. Pigott and Son as *Lady Vera*
1969 : sold to W. E. White, London as *Lash White*
1973 : sold to Thames Serv. Maritime, London as
: *Turbulent*
1974 : scrapped

BUREAUCRAT (1921-1967)
built : 1916
yard : Cochrane and Sons Ltd, Selby
1921 : purchased from Mr. T. C. Spink
1967 : scrapped at Belgium

CHESTER (1921-1922)
built : 1900
yard :
1921 : purchased from Humber Steam Towing
: Co.
1922 : sold

DALESMAN (1921-1936)
built : 1909
yard : Henry Scarr Ltd, Hessle
15.4.21 : purchased from T. Gray
1936 : scrapped at Inverkeithing

DOCKMAN (1963-1973)
built : 1949
yard : Henry Scarr Ltd, Hessle
1963 : purchased as *Stamford Brook*
1973 : sold to Wm. Cory, London as *Dockman*
19.. : sold as *Regal*
19.. : sold to Tyne Towage, Dunston as *Dockman*
1992 : sold to Survey & Supply, Grimsby

ELSA PARTISS (1954-1959)
built : 1908
yard :
1954 : purchased from Foster Tow
1959 : scrapped

ENGLISHMAN (1) (1921-1932)
built : 1913
yard : Henry Scarr Ltd, Hessle
15.4.21 : purchased from T. Gray and Co.
1932 : sold to His Highness Mirza Husain
: Yaverkhan, Saheb Bhahadur, Nawab of
: Cambay India as *Kimiadad*

ENGLISHMAN (2) (1937-1941)
built : 1937
yard : Cochrane and Sons Ltd, Selby
8.9.39 : requisitioned by Min. of Shipping
21.1.41 : 40 miles off Tory Island destroyed by
: German fighters

ENGLISHMAN (3) (1947-1962)
built : 1945
yard : Cochrane and Sons Ltd, Selby
1945-1947 : Admiralty — *Enchanter* (W 178)
27.7.47 : purchased by U.T.L.
1962 : sold to Supreme Cia Nav. S.A. Portugal as
: *Cintra*

Aquilla.

Hullman (1)

124

Englishman (1)

Guardsman (1)

1968   : sold to Tsavliris Ltd, Piraeus as *Nisos*
           : *Skiathos*
1972   : scrapped

ENGLISHMAN (4) (1962-1963)

built   : 1945
yard   : Henry Robb Ltd, Leith
1945-1962 : Royal Navy — *Reward* (Bustler Class)
1962-1963 : chartered by U.T.L. (10.5.62—2.6.63)
10.8.76   : sank after collision; raised and sold for scrap

ENGLISHMAN (5) (1965-1980)

built   : 1965
yard   : Cochrane and Sons Ltd, Selby
1980   : sold to Italy as *Jumbo Primo*
1993   : sold to T.S.A. Tugs as *Towing Witch*

EUROMAN (1) (1972-1976)

built   : 1967
yard   : A. G. Weser, Bremerhaven
1967-1972 : *Bremen* — Unterweser Rederei,
           : Bremerhaven
1972   : purchased by U.T.L.
1976   : sold to J. Latsis, Piraeus as *Petrolas*
           : *Oceanmaster XXIV*
19..   : renamed *Petrolas Oceanmaster 24*

EUROMAN (2) (1982-1986)

built   : 1978
1978-1982 : *Norman Rock* — Solstad
1982-1982 : *ITL Anna B.* — U.T.L.
1982   : chartered by U.T.L. renamed *Euroman*
1986   : sold to U.T.L. as *Anna B.*
1988   : renamed *ITL Anna B.*
1988   : sank

FENMAN (1) (1921-1928)

built   : 1880
yard   : Mr. Watson, Gainsborough
15.4.21   : purchased from T. Gray and Co.
2.1.28   : sold to F. Hall & Co. as *Halls Laddie*

FENMAN (2) (1953-1963)

built   : 1943

yard   : Richard Dunston Ltd, Thorne
1943-1952 : Min. of War Transport *TID 47*
1952-1953 : Lloyds Albert Yard and Master Packet
           : Steam Services Ltd, S'hampton *Ashford 47*
17.4.53   : purchased as *Ashford 47*
10.3.53   : sank 1953
18.5.54   : back in service with U.T.L.
1963   : scrapped at Maassluis

FERRYMAN (1926-1942)

built   : 1914
yard   : N.V. Machinefabriek Bolnes, Holland
1926   : purchased from Thompson Towage
           : (ex *Tormentor*)
23.11.42 : requisitioned by the Royal Navy
2.10.45   : registry cancelled

FINLEY (1921-1929)

built   : 1914
yard   : Scott and Sons, Bowling
1914   : R. H. Mungall, Hessle
30.4.21   : purchased from Premier Tug Co. Ltd.
1929   : sold to Dock & Harb. Comm. Boston
1968   : sold to Ireland

FOREMAN (1959-1972)

built   : 1959 — First sea-going motor tug
yard   : Cook Welton and Gemmell, Beverley
1972   : sold to C. J. King, Bristol as *Sea Bristolian*
1981   : sold to Mustafa en Najabi & Co. Dubai as
           : *Manco*
2.10.81   : struck the rocks near Montalvo Beach on
           : delivery voyage

FORTO (1968-1968)

built   : 1930
yard   : Cook Welton and Gemmell, Beverley
13.3.68   : purchased from Ellerman Line Ltd. Hull
24.6.68   : registry cancelled and broken up

FRENCHMAN (1921-1928)

built   : 1892 as *Coquet*
yard   : J. P. Rennoldson and Son, South Shields

```
1899-1921 :  T. Gray and Co.
1906       :  lengthened
25.4.21    :  purchased
1921-1929 :  used as passenger vessel
1929       :  engine removed and used as a steel dump
           :  barge
1963       :  sold for scrap
1968       :  scrapped
```

GUARDSMAN (1) (1921-1940)
```
built      :  1905
yard       :  Ailsa Shipbuilding Co. Ltd, Ayr
15.4.21    :  purchased from T. Gray and Co.
28.8.39    :  requisitioned for war service
15.11.40   :  struck a mine near N. Foreland and sank
```

GUARDSMAN (2) (1947-1967)
```
built      :  1946
yard       :  Cochrane and Sons Ltd, Selby
1946-1947 :  Min. of War Transport Empire Nina
10.3.47    :  purchased by U.T.L. and renamed
           :  Guardsman
1967       :  scrapped
```

GUARDSMAN (3) (1976-1980)
```
built      :  1976
yard       :  Jonker and Stans, Hendrik Ido Ambacht,
           :  Holland
1980       :  sold to Alianza Nav. Argentina S.A. as
           :  Alianza San Nicolas
```

GUARDSMAN (4) (1989-1992)
```
built      :  1977
1977-1988 :  OSA — Hirtenturm
1988-1989 :  sold to unknown owners as Cape May
1989       :  purchased by U.T.L. and renamed
           :  Guardsman
1992       :  sold to Ocean Finaval Offshore, Trieste as
           :  Odin
```

HANDYMAN(1) 1921-1936
```
built      :  1909
yard       :  Cook Welton and Gemmell, Beverley
```

```
15.4.21    :  purchased from T. Gray and Co.
1936       :  scrapped
```

HEADMAN (1)(1924-1962)
```
built      :  1924
yard       :  Cochrane and Sons Ltd, Selby
23.1.62    :  sold to Lawson Batey, Newcastle as Hillsider
1972       :  scrapped
```

HEADMAN (2) (1963-1978)
```
built      :  1963
yard       :  Cochrane and Sons Ltd, Selby
1.4.78     :  transferred to Humber Tugs
1981       :  sold to Alex Tsavliris & Sons Piraeus as
           :  Hermes
```

HILLMAN (1930-1938)
```
built      :  1930
yard       :  Henry Scarr Ltd, Hessle
22.3.38    :  sold to Venezuelan Oil Development Co.
           :  Ltd. as Esperanza
```

HULLMAN (1) (1921-1928)
```
built      :  1914
yard       :  Hepple and Co. South Shields
15.4.21    :  purchased from T. Gray and Co.
1928       :  sold to Antigosti Shipping Corporation,
           :  Montreal
1932       :  sold to Manseau Shipyards Ltd, Sorel
           :  Quebec
```

HULLMAN (2) (1968-1972)
```
built      :  1968
yard       :  C. D. Holmes and Co. Ltd, Beverley
1972       :  sank in the North Sea
```

IONA (1921-1958)
```
built      :  1905
yard       :  Henry Scarr Ltd, Hessle
19.7.14    :  sold to Premier Tug Co. Ltd. to
           :  W. H. Miller
30.4.21    :  purchased from T. Gray and Co.
1958       :  scrapped
```

Mabel.

Biddy.

IRISHMAN (1) (1921-1926)
built   : 1900
yard   :
1921   : purchased from T. Gray and Co.
1926   : sold to J. Deheer, Hull as *Ian*

IRISHMAN (2) (1929-1961)
built   : 1929
yard   : Cochrane and Sons Ltd, Selby
1941   : struck a mine near Portsmouth
1961   : sold to Italy as *Genaggentu*

IRISHMAN (3) (1967-1976)
built   : 1967
yard   : Cochrane and Sons Ltd, Selby
1.4.74   : transferred to Star Offshore Services
1976   : sold to Guybulk Shipping, Hamilton as
          : *Kwakwani*
1978   : sold to ITL. Rochester as *Lorna-B*
1981   : sold to Standard Towing Ltd. Vancouver as
          : *Pacific Standard*

IRISHMAN (4) (1978-1987)
built   : 1978
yard   : Cochrane and Sons Ltd, Selby
1987   : sold to Semco, Singapore as *Salvision*
1993   : sold to Pacific Carriers, Singapore as
          : *Pacnav Ace*

JAMES WATT (1921-1929)
built   : 1858
yard   : Harrison and Laurence, Hull
1904-1921 : T. Gray and Co.
15.4.21   : purchased by U.T.L.
1929   : sold to Lincoln and Hull Water Transport
          : Co. Ltd.
1935   : scrapped

KEELMAN (1962-1978)
built   : 1958
yard   : P. K. Harris and Sons Ltd, Appledore
1962   : purchased as *Scorcher* — Royal Navy
1.4.78   : transferred to Humber Tugs

KINSMAN (1921-1930)
built   : 1908
yard   : Cook Welton and Gemmell, Beverley
1921   : purchased from T. Gray and Co.
1930   : sold to J. P. Knight as *Keverne*
1946   : sold to D. Vernicos, Piraeus as *Vernicos Eleni*

KROOMAN (1) (1921-1936)
built   : 1905
yard   : J. P. Rennoldson and Son, South Shields
1921   : purchased from T. Gray and Co.
1936   : scrapped at Inverkeithing

KROOMAN (2) (1938-1973)
built   : 1938
yard   : Cochrane and Sons Ltd, Selby
25.8.39   : requisitioned
29.6.63   : sank near Hull; raised
1965   : re-engined into Diesel
29.5.73   : sold to Greece as *Jason*
1988   : scrapped

LADY BUTE (1921-1924)
built   : 1857
yard   : unknown at Cardiff
1921   : purchased from T. Gray and Co.
1924   : scrapped

LADY CONSTANCE (1982   )
built   : 1982
yard   : Cochrane and Sons Ltd, Selby

LADY DEBBIE (1978-   )
built   : 1978
yard   : Cochrane and Sons Ltd, Selby

LADY ELIZABETH (1981-   )
built   : 1981
yard   : Cochrane and Sons Ltd, Selby

LADY MOIRA (1977-
built   : 1977
yard   : Cochrane and Sons Ltd, Selby

LADY SYBIL (1987-   )
built   : 1987
yard   : Cochrane and Sons Ltd, Selby

LADY THERESA (1988-   )
built   : 1988
yard   : Cochrane and Sons Ltd, Selby

LANCELOT (1961-1962)
built   : ?
yard   :
1961   : purchased from Foster Tow, Hull
1962   : scrapped

LARKSPUR (1961-1962)
built   : 1919
yard   :
1919-1952 : Royal Navy — Royal Navy
1961   : purchased from Foster Tow, Hull
1962   : scrapped

LIGHTERMAN (1) (1929-1955)
built   : 1917
yard   :
1929   : purchased from the Admiralty as *AT 144*
1955   : scrapped

LIGHTERMAN (2) (1962-1977)
built   : 1954
yard   : P. K. Harris, Appledore
28.2.62   : purchased as *Jaycee*
20.8.77   : sold to Felixarc Marine Ltd, Felixstowe as
          : *Gary Gray*
1984   : chartered to Satim Towage, Ipswich
1988   : sold to Heysham

LINESMAN (1) (1921-1962)
built   : 1922
yard   : J. P. Rennoldson and Son, South Shields
1921   : purchased from T. Gray and Co.
1962   : scrapped at Rotterdam

LINESMAN (2) (1976-1979)
built   : 1976
1979   : sold to Alianza Nav. Argentinië S.A. as
          : *Alianza Campana*

LLOYDSMAN (1971-1979)
built   : 1971

yard   : Henry Robb, Leith
3.10.79   : sold to Selco, Singapore as *Salviscount*
1988   : scrapped

MABEL (1921-1956)
built   : 1890
yard   : Westwood Baillie and Co. London Yard
          : Poplar
23.3.21   : purchased from T. C. Spink
1956   : scrapped

MARKSMAN (1921-1964)
built   : 1914
yard   : J. P. Rennoldson and Son, South Shields
15.4.21   : purchased from T. Gray and Co.
14.10.64 : registry cancelled

MASTERMAN (1) (1923-1925)
built   : 1923
yard   : Cochrane and Sons Ltd, Selby
10.2.25   : sold to George Edgley, Gravesend as
          : *Watercock*
1966   : scrapped

MASTERMAN (2) (1946-1961)
built   : 1941
yard   : Goole Shipbuilding and Repairing Co. Ltd
1941-1946 : Min. of War Transport - *Empire Larch*
1961   : sold to Brodospas, Split as *Smjeli*
1972   : scrapped

MASTERMAN (3) (1964-1985)
built   : 1964
yard   : C. D. Holmes, Beverley
1969   : sold to Universal Trawlers
1973   : back in service with U.T.L. and transferred
          : to Humber Tugs
1985   : sold to Holyhead Towing as *Afon Wen*
1986   : back in service with U.T.L. as *Masterman*
1986   : sold to Hellenic Tugs as *Ektor*

MERCHANTMAN (1) (1946-1962)
built   : 1945
yard   : Clelands Ltd, Wallsend

Pinky.

Bureaucrat.

1945-1946 : Min. of War Transport *Empire Bess*
1946 : purchased by U.T.L.
1962 : sold to Soc. Arm. Napolitani, Naples as
: *Tarentum*
1981 : scrapped

MERCHANTMAN (1964-1967)
built : 1964
yard : C. D. Holmes Ltd, Beverley
19.9.67 : sank in the North Sea

MERMAN (1921-1962)
built : 1911
yard : J. P. Rennoldson and Son, South Shields
1921 : purchased from T. Gray and Co.
1962 : scrapped at Rotterdam

MOORSMAN (1972-)
built : 1975
yard : Dredge and Marine Ltd. Ponsharden Ship
: yard, Penryn

MOTORMAN (1) (1925-1955)
built : 1925
yard : Henry Scarr Ltd, Hessle
1955 : scrapped

MOTORMAN (2) (1965-1978)
built : 1965
yard : Humber St. Andrews Engineering Co. Ltd.
: Hull
4.4.78 : transferred to Humber Tugs
8.12.83 : sold to Klyne & Winney, Lowestoft as
: *Anglian Man*
1988 : sold to G. Beezley, Hartlepool as
: *Clevelandman*
1988 : sold to Colne Shipping, Lowestoft as *Eta*

MUSCOVITE (1921-1930)
built : 1882
yard : Unsune et Chantiers de la Seine, Arcenteuil
1918 : purchased by John Watt and R. W.
: Wheeldon as *Pilote*
20.1.21 : purchased from T. C. Spink and Co.

1930 : sold to J. Deheer Ltd, Hull
1950 : scrapped

NOBLEMAN (1925-1937)
built : 1925
yard : Cochrane and Sons Ltd, Selby
7.9.37 : sold to Falmouth Tow Co. Ltd, Falmouth
: as *Fairnile*
1959 : renamed *St. Agnes*
1959 : registry cancelled

NORMAN (1) (1921-1926)
built : 1897
yard : H. Fellow and Son, Yarmouth
1921 : purchased from T. Gray and Co.
1926 : scrapped

NORMAN (2) (1929-1972)
built : 1929
yard : Cochrane and Sons Ltd, Selby
1941-1943 : Royal Navy *Diversion*
1954 : re-engined into diesel
1972 : scrapped at Hull

NORMAN (3) (1973-1975)
built : 1968
yard : Cochrane and Sons Ltd, Selby
1968-1973 : McDermott Offshore — *Jaramac XXVIII*
1.4.74 : transferred to Star Offshore Services
13.12.75 : sank off the Humber

ORION (1921-1926)
built : 1900
yard :
1921 : purchased from City Steam Towing Co.
: Hull
1926 : scrapped

OVERGARTH (1961-1961)
built : 1907
yard :
1961 : purchased from Foster Tow, Hull
1961 : scrapped

PATROLMAN (1963-1972)

built	:	1953
yard	:	Henry Scarr Ltd, Hessle
1963	:	purchased as *Colne Brook* (ex *Brook*)
1972	:	sold to Greece as *Kampos*

PINKY (1921-1964)

built	:	1916
yard	:	Livingstone and Cooper, Hessle
30.4.21	:	purchased from Premier Tug Co. Ltd.
1964	:	scrapped at Queensborough

PIONEER (1921-1924)

built	:	1906
yard	:	P. McGregor and Sons, Kirkintilloch
1906-1909	:	Pioneer Tug and Lighter Co.
1909-1913	:	William Gilyott and Co. Hull
1913-1921	:	R. W. Wheeldon
15.4.21	:	purchased by U.T.L.
4.3.24	:	sold to P. Foster Tugs, Hull
1938	:	scrapped

POWERFUL (1921-1925)

built	:	1875
yard	:	
1921	:	purchased from S. Harrison, Hull
1925	:	scrapped

PRESSMAN (1) (1927-1938)

built	:	1923
yard	:	Cochrane and Sons Ltd, Selby
23.10.27	:	purchased from Thompson Towage as *Torris*
1938	:	sold to Soc. An. Les Goelands, Oran as *Goeland II*

PRESSMAN (2) (1963-1972)

built	:	1950
yard	:	
1963	:	purchased as *Tyburn Brook*
1972	:	sold to M. E. Street, Bullart & King as *Presstan*
1984	:	sold to Eddie Carney, Clyde
19..	:	sold to J. Dean, Hull as *Presstan*

PRESTO (1968-1968)

built	:	1943
yard	:	Cochrane and Sons Ltd, Selby
1943-1946	:	Min. of War Transport *Empire Sarah*
15.6.46	:	purchased by Ellerman's Wilson Line
13.3.68	:	purchased from Ellerman Lines, Hull
24.6.68	:	registry cancelled and broken up

PRIZEMAN (1925-1972)

built	:	1925
yard	:	Cochrane and Sons Ltd, Selby
28.5.37	:	sank in the Humber and raised
1954	:	re-engined into diesel
1972	:	scrapped at Hull

R. W. WHEELDON (1921-1948)

built	:	1912
yard	:	Kaldnaes Patent Ship and Mek Vaerksted,
	:	Tonsberg
6.9.20	:	purchased in Norway by R. W. Wheeldon
	:	as *Cabral*
15.4.21	:	purchased from City Steam Towing Co.
	:	Hull
1948	:	scrapped

RIFLEMAN (1947-1967)

built	:	1945
yard	:	Cochrane and Sons Ltd, Selby
1945-1947	:	Min. of War Transport *Empire Vera*
28.7.47	:	purchased by U.T.L.
1967	:	scrapped

RIVERMAN (1) (1926-1948)

built	:	1915
yard	:	de Groot en van Vliet, Slikkerveer, Holland
23.10.26	:	purchased from Thompson Tow, Hull as
	:	*Traho*
1948	:	scrapped

RIVERMAN (2) (1963-1974)

built	:	1963
yard	:	Drypool Engineering and Dry Dock Co.
	:	Ltd, Hull
1974	:	sold to Haugesund, Norway as *Torian*

Motorman.

Pressman.

RIVERMAN (3) (1974-   )
built   : 1955 see *BARGEMAN*

ROMAN (1921-1961)
built   : 1906
yard   : J. P. Rennoldson and Son, South Shields
15.4.21   : purchased from T. Gray and Co.
28.8.39   : requisitioned for war service
1961   : scrapped at Gateshead

ROMULUS (1926-1927)
built   : 1883
yard   :
1926   : purchased from Thompson Towage Hull
1927   : scrapped

SALVAGEMAN (1980-1989)
built   : 1980 originally named *Nobleman*
yard   : Chung Wah Shipbuilding & Engineering
             : Co. Ltd, Hong Kong
1989   : sold to Cosmar, Spanje as *Hispania*
             : *Anglian Prince*

SCOTSMAN (1) (1926-1927)
built   : 1903 voor T. Gray and Co.
yard   : Cook Welton and Gemmell, Hull
1919   : sold to All. Seas Marine & Salv. Co. Ltd.
             : Halifax
1923   : sold to Thompson Tow, Hull
23.10.26   : purchased by U.T.L.
11.2.27   : certificate cancelled

SCOTSMAN (2) (1929-1972)
built   : 1929
yard   : Cochrane and Sons Ltd, Selby
1954   : re-engined into diesel
1972   : scrapped at Hull

SCOTSMAN (3) (1973-1981)
built   : 1969
yard   : Cochrane and Sons Ltd, Selby
1969-1972   : *E. Bronson Ingram*
1972-1973   : McDermott *Jaramac 42*
1973   : purchased by U.T.L.

1974   : transferred to Star Offshore Services
1981   : sold to McDermott, Saudi Arabia as
             : *Al Battal*
1987   : sold to Lake Ontario Cement Co. as *Petite*
             : *Forte*

SEAMAN (1) (1924-1964)
built   : 1924
             : Made the first company's first ocean tow in
             : 1925
yard   : Cochrane and Sons Ltd, Selby
1939-1944   : requisitioned by Royal Navy, renamed
             : *Seaman* (W-44)
1964   : scrapped at Queensborough

SEAMAN (2) (1967-1978)
built   : 1967
yard   : Cochrane and Sons Ltd, Selby
1978   : sold to Venecia Shipping Serv. Puerto
             : Cabello, Venezuela as *Vesca R 5*

SEAMAN (3) (1984-1990)
built   : 1984
yard   :
1990   : sold to Rimor. Riuniti, Genoa as *Genua*

SEEKER (1920-1958)
built   : 1913
yard   :
1913-1920   : *Vier je sleep*
1920   : purchased from Foster Tow, Hull
1958   : scrapped

SERVICEMAN (1) (1946-1969)
built   : 1945
yard   : Cochrane and Sons Ltd, Selby
1945-1946   : Min. of War Transport *Empire Stella*
1946   : purchased by U.T.L.
1961   : re-engined
1969   : sold to Italy as *Poetto*

SERVICEMAN (2) (1976-1979)
built   : 1976
yard   : Ijsselwerf B.V. Rotterdam

1979	:	sold to Alianza Nav. Argentina S.A. as
	:	*Alianza San Pedro*
1982	:	sold to Homero Fonda y Cia. as *Albatros I*
1992	:	renamed *Albatros III*
1993	:	chartered by Wijsmuller, Holland

SINDIA (1926-1930)

built	:	1917 as *H.S. '64*
yard	:	Crabtree and Co. Ltd, Great Yarmouth
1926	:	purchased from Thompson Tow, Hull and
	:	renamed *Tribesman*
1930	:	sold to Le Havre

SOUTHERN CROSS (1921-1936)

built	:	1896
yard	:	Henry Scarr Ltd, Beverley
15.4.21	:	purchased from City Steam Towing Co.
1936	:	scrapped at Inverkeithing

STATESMAN (1969-1978)

built	:	1966
yard	:	Kure Shipbuilding and Engineering Co.
	:	Japan
1966-1969	:	*Alice L. Moran* — Moran Towing
1969-1973	:	in charter with U.T.L.
1973	:	purchased by U.T.L. and renamed
	:	*Statesman I*
1978	:	renamed *Statesman*
15.8.78	:	sold to Selco, Singapore, as *Salvanguard*
1986	:	chartered by Wijsmuller as *Amsterdam*
1988	:	layed up in Persian Gulf

STEPHEN GRAY (1921-1928)

built	:	1882
yard	:	E. Wales, Groves, Hull
15.4.21	:	purchased from T. Gray and Co.
1928	:	scrapped at Inverkeithing

SUPERMAN (1) (1923-1928)

built	:	1923
yard	:	Cochrane and Sons Ltd, Selby (first new
	:	built vessel in the fleet)
28.7.28	:	sold to Angel Gardella B. Aires as *Juan Jose*
1939	:	renamed *Celso-R*

SUPERMAN (2) (1933-1964)

built	:	1933
yard	:	Cochrane and Sons Ltd, Selby
1939-1945	:	requisitioned by the Royal Navy, renamed
	:	*Superman* (W-89)
1964	:	scrapped at Queensborough

SUPERMAN (3) (1967-1969)

built	:	1967
yard	:	C. D. Holmes Ltd, Beverley
1969	:	sold to Venecia Shipping Serv, Venezuela
	:	as *Vesca R-6*

TERRIER (1926-1926)

built	:	1883
yard	:	
1926	:	purchased from Thompson Towage, Hull
1926	:	scrapped

THEMIS (1921-1924)

built	:	1909
yard	:	Cox and Co. Falmouth
1909-1921	:	R. W. Wheeldon
15.4.21	:	purchased from City Steam Towing Co.
	:	Hull
12.2.24	:	sold to Foster Tugs, Hull
1951	:	sold abroad and condemned at Freetown

TIDESMAN (1963-1981)

built	:	1963
yard	:	Humber St. Andrews Engineering Co. Ltd.
1978	:	transferred to Humber Tugs
1981	:	sold to Alex G. Tsavliris & Sons Piraeus as
	:	*Hector*

TOLLMAN (1931-1966)

built	:	1931
yard	:	Henry Scarr Ltd, Hessle
23.5.62	:	sank near Hull
26.6.62	:	raised
1966	:	registry cancelled

TORMENTOR (1926-1942)

| built | : | 1914 |

Scotsman.

Krooman.

yard   :
1926   : purchased from Thompson Towage Hull
        : renamed *Ferryman*
1942   : transferred to His Majesty
1945   : no longer in the register

TORRIS (1926-1938)
built   : 1923
yard   :
1926   : purchased from Thompson Towage Hull,
        : renamed *Pressman*
1938   : sold to Soc. An Les Goeland Oran as
        : *Goeland II*

TRACKER (1915-1922)
built   : 1915
yard   :
1922   : sold to Crown

TRADESMAN (1) (1924-1928)
built   : 1924
yard   : Cochrane and Sons Ltd, Selby
1928   : sold to Cia. Argentina de Nav. Dodero
        : Buenos Aires as *Mediator*

TRADESMAN (2) (1946-1963)
built   : 1944
yard   : Clelands Ltd. Willington, Tyne
1944-1946 : Min. of War Transport *Empire Julia*
1946   : purchased by U.T.L.
1963   : sold to Vernicos, Piraeus as *Vernicos Kitty*
1973   : scrapped

TRADESMAN (3) (1964-1977)
built   : 1964
yard   : C. D. Holmes and Co. Ltd, Beverley
26.5.72 : sold to J. H. Pigott renamed *Lady Joan*
9.5.77 : returned to U.T.L.
1.6.77 : transferred to Humber Tugs
1977   : renamed *Lady Joan*
1985   : sold to Sargenavi, Naples as *Salernum*

TRAHO (1926-1948)
built   : 1915

yard   :
1926   : purchased from Thompson Towage, Hull
        : and renamed *Riverman*
1948   : scrapped

TRAWLERMAN (1963-1986)
built   : 1963
yard   : Humber St. Andrews Engineering Co. Ltd,
        : Hull
1983   : transferred to Humber Tugs
17.11.85 : sold to Roger and Bridget Klyne, Lowestoft

TRIBESMAN (1926-1930)
built   : 1917 see *Sindia*

TUGMAN (1964-1983)
built   : 1964
yard   : Humber St. Andrews Engineering Co. Ltd,
        : Hull
1.4.78 : transferred to Humber Tugs
24.8.83 : sold to Klyne Winney, Lowestoft, as *Anglian*
1988   : sold to G. Brindley, Lowestoft
1994   : sold to J. Dean, Hull as *Anglian*

TYRE (1921-1926)
built   : 1888
yard   : James F. Gibb, Ratcliff
1913   : purchased by Troy Steam Towing, Hull
2.3.21 : purchased by U.T.L.
1926   : scrapped

VICTOR (1921-1924)
built   : 1876
yard   : J. Eltringham, South Shields
2.5.21 : purchased from Troy Steam Towing, Hull
1924   : scrapped at Felixstowe

WATERMAN (1) (1930-1963)
built   : 1930
yard   : Cochrane and Sons Ltd, Selby
1963   : scrapped at Hull

WATERMAN (2) (1966-1977)
built   : 1966

yard : Richard Dunston Ltd, Thorne
1977 : sold to Norway as *Waterchief*

WELSHMAN (1) (1921-1953)
built : 1896
yard : J. P. Rennoldson and Son, South Shields
15.4.21 : purchased from T. Gray, Hull
1953 : scrapped

WELSHMAN (2) (1958-1963)
built : 1943
yard : Henry Robb, Leith
1943-1952 : *Caroline Moller*
1952-1954 : *Castle Peak*
1954-1958 : Royal Navy — *Growler*
1958 : purchased by U.T.L.
1963 : back to Secr. of State Defence as *Ciclone*
1983 : sold to Shipmarc Ltd, Kenia as *Martial*
1985 : scrapped

WELSHMAN (3) (1966-1978)
built : 1966
yard : Cochrane and Sons Ltd, Selby yard
1974 : transferred to Star Offshore Services
1978 : sold to J. P. Knight, Rochester as *Kinluce*
1988 : sold to Klyne Winney, Lowestoft as
: *Anglian Lady II*
1992 : sold to Remolques del Atlantico Remay,
Spanje as *Vikingo*
1992 : sold to Puertos y Obras, La Coruna as
: *Kochab*

WINCHMAN (1976-1979)
built : 1976
yard :
1979 : sold to Alianza Nav. Argentina as *Alianza*
: *Rosario*

WINCHESTER (1921-1926)
built : 1900
yard :
1921 : purchased from Humber Steam Towing

: Co. Hull
1926 : scrapped

WORKMAN (1963-1979)
built : 1963
yard : Cochrane and Sons Ltd, Selby
1.4.78 : transferred to Humber Tugs
16.1.79 : sold to Wenhove Ltd. Aberdeen as *Duncan*
1980 : sold to F. Pearce, Poole as *Pullwell Delta*
1985 : sold to Oil Transport Co, Panama as *OTC*
: *Elizabeth*

YEOMAN (1953-1963)
built : 1944
yard : Richard Dunston Ltd, Thorne
1944-1953 : Min. of War Transport — *TID 90*
1953-1953 : Lloyds Alert Yard and Motor Packet
: Services Ltd. Southampton *Ashford 90*
23.9.53 : purchased by U.T.L.
1963 : scrapped at Hendrik Ido Ambacht

YORKSHIREMAN (1) (1928-1965)
built : 1928
yard : Earles Shipbuilding and Engineering Co.
: Ltd, Hull
6.10.39 : requisitioned for War Service
1965 : scrapped at Belgium

YORKSHIREMAN (2) (1967-1974)
built : 1967
yard : C. D. Holmes Ltd, Beverley
1974 : transferred to Humber Tugs as *Lady*
: *Theresa*
1981 : sold to Tsavliris as *Atlas*

YORKSHIREMAN (1978-1987)
built : 1978
yard : Cochrane and Sons Ltd, Selby
1987 : chartered to Semco, Singapore
1988 : sold to Semco, Singapore as *Salvigour*
1989 : sold to Reboques Fluviales do Sado,
: Portugal as *Comenda*

Norman.

Serviceman.

143

Foreman.

Autocrat towing the **Whitby Abbey**.

Norman working on the River Humber.

Norseman.

Bowman *docking the* **Whitby Abbey**.

Bargeman.

Keelman.

147

Tradesman.

Nobleman.

Serviceman, Guardsman, Fenman
*and **Rifleman**.*

Motorman.

Presto.

Lady Moira.

Yorkshireman leaving Hull for the breaker's yard.

Lancelot towing the **Kingston Pearl**.

Scotsman.

Working off the jetty by King George Dock.

THE UNITED TOWING STAFF — 1990

M. J. Lacey,
Managing Director
since 1981

Capt. Norman Storey OBE,
Marine/Towing Superintendent,
Joined 1948, came ashore 1977.

Capt. Mark Hoddinott,
Salvage Superintendent,
Joined 1982.

Alison Pickard,
Secretary to Managing Director,
Joined 1973.

Capt. Dennis Pearce,
Senior Salvage Superintendent,
Joined 1975.

Capt. Eric Johnson,
Salvage Superintendent,
Joined Humber Tugs 1966,
Transferred to United Towing 1983.

Paul Escreet,
Commercial Director,
Joined 1972.

Captain Mark Hoddinott
Salvage Superintendent

Paul Escreet
Commercial Director

Captain Eric Johnson
Salvage Superintendent

Alison Pickard
Secretary to Managing Director

Captain Dennis Pearce
Senior Salvage Superintendent

Captain Norman Storey O.B.E.
Marine/Towing Superintendent